The Awesomely Awful '80s,
Part 2

Apocalypse Later
Books by Hal C. F. Astell

<u>Annual Series</u>
A Hundred in 2016

<u>Awesomely Series</u>
The Awesomely Awful '80s, Part 2

<u>Cinematic Hell Series</u>
Huh? An A-Z of Why Classic American Bad Movies Were Made

<u>Festival Series</u>
The International Horror & Sci-Fi Film Festival: The Transition Years

<u>Filmography Series</u>
Velvet Glove Cast in Iron: The Films of Tura Satana
Charlie Chaplin Centennial: Keystone

Apocalypse Later
Awesomely Series

The Awesomely Awful '80s, Part 2

APOCALYPSE LATER

Apocalypse Later Awesomely Series
The Awesomely Awful '80s, Part 2

ISBN-10: 0-9894613-6-X

ISBN-13: 978-0-9894613-6-8

Apocalypse Later Press catalogue number: ALP006

Text by Hal C. F. Astell

Some of these reviews appeared in evolutionary form at Apocalypse Later Film Reviews or Apocalypse Later Now!

https://www.apocalypselaterfilm.com/
https://www.apocalypselaternow.blogspot.com/

Cover art by April Reyna of Reyna Art

https://www.instagram.com/reyna_art/

Graphic design by Jason Drotman of Steamheart Design

https://www.steamheart.com/

All posters reproduced here are believed to be owned either by the studios, producers or distributors of their associated films, or the graphic artists or photographers who originally created them. They, along with all screenshots, are used here for the purpose for which they were intended in reduced, black and white form in accordance with fair use or dealing laws.

Typeset in Gentium Plus

https://software.sil.org/gentium/

Published through Kindle Direct Publishing

https://kdp.amazon.com

Licensed through Creative Commons
Attribution-NonCommercial-ShareAlike 3.0 Unported (CC BY-NC-SA 3.0)

https://creativecommons.org/licenses/by-nc-sa/3.0/

Published by Apocalypse Later Press

https://press.apocalypselaterempire.com/

Dedication

To all my fellow Awesomelys who have shared the stage over the years, in chronological order: the Brass Bells, who began the whole thing; Jim *"They Live"* Miller; Heather *"V"* Rice (R.I.P.); Michael *"Pee-wee"* Flanders; Nick *"Nuke 'Em High"* Perillo; Liz *"Hey Dude"* Manning; Britt *"Gummi Bears"* Rhuart; and Alyssa *"Labyrinth"* Provan.

You are all the very definition of awesomely bitchin'!

Acknowledgements

Usually, my acknowledgements begin with my better half, Dee Astell, who gets to see all these films with me and still hasn't killed me for it. This is no exception, but joint first this time out is the Awesomelys audience.

It's still surreal to realise that some of you come to events of the scale of Phoenix ~~Comicon~~ ~~Comic Fest~~ Fan Fusion to see us first and foremost, with everything else—the guests, the vendors, the cosplay—all an added bonus.

You have been behind us since moment one and I salute you!

See you at the next panel!

Contents

Introduction	9

1985 — 15

Remo Williams: The Adventure Begins — 16
Crimewave — 26
The Last Dragon — 36
Water — 46
Gymkata * — 56

1986 — 67

Back to School — 68
Howard the Duck * — 78
Maximum Overdrive — 88
Solarbabies — 98
Trick or Treat — 106

1987 — 117

The Gate * — 118
Adventures in Babysitting — 126
Hard Ticket to Hawaii — 136
Deathstalker II — 146
Blind Date — 154

1988 163

Bloodsport * 164
Hell Comes to Frogtown 174
Dead Heat * 182
Hollywood Chainsaw Hookers 192
Action Jackson 202

1989 215

The Horror Show 216
The Wizard 226
Robot Jox * ° 236
See No Evil, Hear No Evil 246
Road House * 256

Bibliography 266
About Hal C. F. Astell 268
About Apocalypse Later 269

* picks at Awesomely panels 2013-2018
° not actually discussed because of the fire alarm incident

Introduction

Somehow the beginnings of the Awesomelys have become shrouded in mystery. Why, I have no idea. This isn't ancient history, after all. We only date back to 2013, but that first year is still something of a blur.

Here's what we know for sure. The Brass Bells, a pair of twins whom I'd never previously met, pitched a panel idea to Phoenix Comicon, then very much in the ascendant. It would be called "Awesomely Awful 80's" and the description that made it into the program guide read as follows:

> "The 80's had a lot of awesomely awful sci-fi TV shows and movies. Remember AutoMan? Remember the movie Howard the Duck? Remember MASK? Join us as we reminisce about the really bad 80's sci-fi that, despite the awfulness, we all love so much."

2013 was the year I published my first two books, including one on the "worst movies of all time", and I'd timed publication so that I'd have the first copies in my hands (and on a variety of friends' tables) at Phoenix Comicon, so I was keen to promote. I reached out to the powers that be at Square Egg Entertainment to see if I could get onto some panels and this one leapt out as a gimme.

Also on the panel, along with the Brass Bells and I, were Jim Miller and Heather Rice. I knew Jim already from the local film scene and he's moved on to a great number of things, including his own gaming retreat, Crit Hit! Heather I didn't know at all but, on arriving at the panel, I was surprised to discover that she was the cousin of a long time friend of the family. Small world, huh?

The format that the Brass Bells came up with was very similar to what we've done in the years since. We panelists picked movies and TV shows and they showed the trailers or opening credits, hoping that the audience would react. They did and, after each, we talked a little about that title and why we saw it as a guilty pleasure.

The mystery is that we don't seem to remember what we picked, how we picked or even what criteria we used. I have a feeling we each picked a movie and the Brass Bells threw in the rest. But those movies! *Howard the Duck* was there in the description, so that must have been the Brass Bells. My pick was *Galaxina*, which was a long term guilty pleasure, a little more obscure than the others; that's something I've continued to do as the years and events have continued. I think Heather's was *Deathstalker* because I do recall commenting on how much more fun its first sequel was.

It was Jim's pick where things really clicked though. He chose *They Live*, John Carpenter's sf action flick with "Rowdy" Roddy Piper, which sparked a fun argument between he and I as to whether it was fair to categorise it as "awful" or not. He clearly thought it was and I conceded the point that any action movie loses credibility when it introduces a suplex into a fight scene. However, I also argued that it's a timeless classic for the ages, a movie that seems to become more and more accurate with each year that passes. Every time I see it, it seems to have become about what I just read in the news the week before.

Jim and I had a lot of fun disagreeing about *They Live* and that, to me, is where the Awesomelys changed from a throwaway pop culture panel at a big pop culture convention to something that I knew I wanted to do on a regular basis. It was certainly the spark for our future expansion into the world of Awesomely Bitchin'!

After that first year, the Brass Bells moved to Portland and I took over what we then called the Awesomelys. Almost everything from that point on is documented on our website: awesomelys.com.

And there's a lot to document!

Our first expansion was in 2014, when we added a second similar panel focused on the '90s. Our second was to a third, Awesomely Bitchin', panel the following year, in which we showcased what we felt were underrated gems or overlooked classics.

There's the sideways shift we made in 2017 to present at an event other than Phoenix Comicon; this was Westercon 70, a regional convention that moves around the western third of North America; my better half chaired it. We debuted a new idea there for an older audience—Awesomely Awful: Across the Decades—in which we looked at films from the '30s to the '00s, something I particularly enjoyed and which we did again at CoKoCon 2018 and have scheduled, as I write, for LepreCon 45, both of which are local science fiction/fantasy conventions.

Finally (so far), there's a zoom in on specific years—1988 and 1998—for Tucson Comic-Con, another new event for us, in 2018. We chose films that were released in the years in question or TV shows that were still on air as part of their original runs.

I should add here that we had planned another expansion at Phoenix Comic Fest in 2018 but circumstances led to it not happening. This was the Audience Picks panel, which we would have held had we not been ushered outside when the fire alarm went off. As the name suggests, we each made our choices from suggestions made by the 2017 audience. We were eager to see how many of our choices had been picked by people still in the audience a year on. Our regulars rock and I wanted to see them respond to our comments about their picks. Well, it didn't happen but it will. It's on the schedule for Phoenix Fan Fusion in 2019.

The website also lists how the group changed over time. My stepson, Michael Flanders, replaced both of the Brass Bells in 2014, and he's been a mainstay ever since. I had seen him on other panels and, while we have different approaches, I learned a lot from him, so he was a natural choice. Even though he started a year later, he's actually done a lot more panels than Jim, who was with us from the very beginning.

Nick Perillo kindly joined us in 2015 after the untimely and unexpected passing of Heather Rice. We really wanted to keep a female voice in the group, though, to keep the perspectives fresh, and we found that in 2016 with Liz Manning, another natural choice given that she's both an actress and a comedienne. Sadly, school kept her busy enough in 2017 for us to need to promote Britt Rhuart to full member instead. He was our supersub in 2016, as he'd stepped into two panels with zero notice to cover for Jim and done a great job. The final personnel change (thus far) has been to add Alyssa Provan to the mix, partly because Jim was running gaming at

The Awesomely Awful '80s, Part 2

Phoenix Comic Fest in 2018 and partly because Britt is in Ohio nowadays, writing theses on exploitation films, and so can't attend events other than Phoenix Comicon, under whichever name it's using this week.

So, all that's documented. What isn't is how long I've wanted to expand in a completely different direction: books.

I have a blast doing Awesomelys panels but I also feel limited. I grew up in the '80s and spent my time immersed in heavy metal, horror fiction and awesomely awful movies. It really is an easy decade for me but I'm very aware that the nostalgia point is rapidly moving from the '80s to the '90s, which I don't know anywhere near as well, especially when it comes to TV. I want to do a '70s panel, but it would warrant a different event with an audience that's slightly older. I'd love to do a '30s panel too, but there are all sorts of problems there, not least that I'm the oldest member of the group and my struggle with the '90s would be echoed in their struggle with the '70s and earlier. It would need to be a films-only panel too, of course, but one driven by whichever movies I can track down trailers for!

The '30s would be much easier to do as a book and I could throw in as many titles as I want, trailer availability be damned! That's a freedom I enjoyed here with my first of hopefully many books in my Awesomelys series. It's all movies, for a start, with no television included at all. It also features five titles from each year of the second half of the '80s, hence the Part 2 when I haven't written a Part 1 yet. That'll come later when I tackle the first half of the '80s. And then it'll be the '30s. Or the '70s. Or *The Return of the Awesomely Awful '80s, Part 2*. I can have a lot of fun with this. I wonder how many Part 2 books I can publish before I write a Part 1!

I certainly want to write more about my primary decade, the '80s. This book only looks at half of it, yet only 7 out of 25 choices have been covered thus far on Awesomely Awful panels. Those other 18 could carry me all the way to Phoenix Fan Fusion 2036 and that's still just scratching the surface!

What I hope you'll find here, though, beyond a glorious nostalgia trip to the decade of big hair and neon spandex and, hopefully, a whole bundle of laughs, is a little insight into how the '80s is a more interesting decade for film than you might think. After all, it saw the boom in home video, which

The Awesomely Awful '80s, Part 2

was a huge opportunity for many filmmakers. Suddenly you didn't need to have millions of dollars, a major studio backing you and a distribution deal for theatrical exhibition. You could just shoot something on video and throw it onto the shelves at Blockbuster. The straight to video world is a glorious one indeed.

Just as we do with our panels, my selections are deliberately varied. It would have been easy to cover 25 horror movies, but genre cinema should never be that limited. Here you'll find science fiction, action, fantasy and comedy in abundance, sometimes all in the same title.

There are films that I saw in the theatre on their original release, like *Bloodsport* and *The Gate*. There are those I picked up on PAL VHS way back in the day, like *Water* and *Deathstalker II*; I wouldn't like to count how many times I've rewound those tapes and watched them over again. And there are films that I somehow missed out on all these years. I hadn't even heard of *Dead Heat* until Britt chose it for Phoenix Comic Fest in 2018 and I hadn't got round to *Robot Jox* until an audience member recommended it, even though I own a punchout plastic poster that I've managed to have signed by co-writer Joe Haldeman and executive producer Charles Band.

I hope you'll find a similar mix: films you know by heart; films you've seen and to which you can enjoy a guilt free return within these pages; and maybe a title or two that you don't know at all but might just have to seek out after you finish this book.

Discovery is always wonderful, even when it's awesomely awful—maybe *especially* when it's awesomely awful!

— Hal C. F. Astell
September 2018

The Awesomely Awful '80s, Part 2

1985

Remo Williams: The Adventure Begins
Crimewave
The Last Dragon
Water
Gymkata

Remo Williams: The Adventure Begins

Director: Guy Hamilton
Writer: Christopher Wood, from the novel by Richard Sapir and Warren Murphy
Stars: Fred Ward, Joel Grey, Wilford Brimley, J. A. Preston, George Coe, Charles Cioffi and Kate Mulgrew

Remo Williams seemed like a perfect place to begin my first Awesomely Awful book, given that it was itself so much of a beginning that it told us so in its very title.

It's an awesomely awful action movie from the decade of awesomely awful action movies, but it's a special one, a series beginner that never got its series, an attempt to bring the *Destroyer* from books to film. If you haven't read any of the 150+ books in the ongoing series, you'll have seen many of them as you pass the "men's adventure" section of any bookstore. It also features an incredible array of talent who slummed it gloriously.

The director is Guy Hamilton, who was responsible for four James Bond movies, including *Goldfinger* and *Live and Let Die*. The star is Fred Ward, an able character actor who's a lot more than just Kevin Bacon's sidekick in *Tremors*: he's played H. P. Lovecraft *and* Ronald Reagan for a start. His co-star, Joel Grey, appearing in yellowface, has won a Oscar, a Tony and a Golden Globe, with two of those for playing the Master of Ceremonies in *Cabaret*. Wilford Brimley is a grumpy old man whose many varied roles range from *Tender Mercies* through *Cocoon* to *The Firm*. And then there's Kate Mulgrew, a full decade before *Star Trek: Voyager*.

That's a rather surprising cast for an action movie in 1985. Who the heck wanted to see an action star who wasn't a bodybuilder or a football player or a professional wrestler. He isn't even a martial arts legend! It's almost like they planned it to be a quality drama, but that's a surprising approach for a film in which an Oscar-winning American singer/dancer literally walks on water while pretending to be Korean.

Fred Ward plays a New York cop, Samuel Edward Makin, who starts out by interrupting a mugging that turns out to be a setup. Two white guys attacking one black guy? Who would have bought that in 1985 New York? Well, Makin takes down all three, but, as he's calling it in, a truck shoves him and his black and white unceremoniously into the East River. And so that's it for Samuel Edward Makin. The driver of the truck even goes to his funeral. Except…

That's right, folks! Sam's alive and mostly well. He's been "recruited by an organisation that doesn't exist". While he was unconscious, they gave him a new face, new fingerprints and even a new name. Now he's Remo Williams, a name conjured up on the fly from the manufacturer's stamp underneath his bedpan. "A lot of thought went into it." They really need his skills as a decorated cop and ex-Marine, who entirely uncoincidentally has no family and no commitments.

Why? Because "everywhere you look, slime is on the loose". The rain that Travis Bickle wanted to wash all the scum off the streets never came; another strike for global warming. The system is corrupt and he's going to be their eleventh commandment: "thou shalt not get away with it". Oh yeah, the dialogue here is all fantastic and it's also delivered deliciously straight by bona fide actors.

And the characters they play are always one step ahead too. When Sam

The Awesomely Awful '80s, Part 2

escapes the hospital by stealing an ambulance, the man who set him up is waiting right behind him with a gun to give him directions. That's Conn McCleary, Mac for short, and he promptly takes him to Harold Smith, who runs this mysterious organisation out of a fake bank through which all the information in the country flows. How big's the organisation? "Just the three of us." So, no ECHELON then; you can put your tinfoil hats away.

Well, the three of them plus the guy Remo Williams is promptly tasked with assassinating. "Remember," says McCleary, handing him a gun. "In. Out. Like a duck mating." Here's where things get truly amazing because this target is Chiun, master of the Korean martial art of Sinanju—all other martial arts are apparently but shadows in comparison—and test number one for Remo, a test that he fails spectacularly. You see, Chiun, who's a thin rake of an old man, can dodge bullets like they're fired in slow motion. He's really a superhero who has no superpowers, just a complete mastery of mind and body, a sort of sexist, racist, anorexic Doc Savage.

Chiun does see some promise in Remo though, even if he does "move like a baboon with two club feet". And so his training begins, which is a real joy because Chiun is a polite psychopath. Mac isn't underestimating things when he warns Remo that, "All I can promise you is terror for breakfast, pressure for lunch and aggravation for sleep."

How, you ask? Well, Chiun has Remo do some crazy obstacle course in his front room, then switches the lights off and has him do it again. He has

him travel all the way round a ferris wheel while hanging on the outside of the car. He has him conquer his fear of heights by standing on the top of the Statue of Liberty's torch. He fires a gun at him at random moments just to see if he can dodge live bullets yet, apparently entirely confident that he'll live through this insane training. "There are times when I could kill you," Remo points out to Chiun. "Good!" replies the master. "We will practice that after dinner!"

Of course, things go well because this wouldn't be much of a movie if they didn't. Before too long, Remo is able to run on sand without leaving footprints, which seems like a pretty good start (and coincidentally pretty useful given that he's tasked with running across wet cement a few scenes later). As Chiun watches his favourite daytime soap opera—America's sole contribution to art, he states—while balancing on his fingers, it has to be said that Remo isn't even batting in the same league yet. Chiun does think Remo will be ready ahead of schedule, though. Fifteen years, if he cuts a few corners.

As much as we enjoy this training, which I would happily watch for an hour and half, there is an actual story here. Smith is investigating George S. Grove, an untouchable defence contractor who's providing sub-quality machine guns to the army and whose proto-Star Wars project, H.A.R.P., is running notably over budget. The very efficient and gutsy Major Rayner Fleming, played by Kate Mulgrew, is also investigating those overruns and

we're in precisely no doubt where we'll end up.

For some reason, *Remo Williams* didn't do too well at the box office and that's a real shame. There are reasons why the *Destroyer* books just keep on coming, after all, and I'd have loved to see more films. Of course, I should confess here that there have been two, neither of which I've seen. *Remo Williams: The Prophecy* was a 1988 TV movie with Roddy McDowall as Chiun and soap opera actor Jeffrey Meek as Remo. Later, in 2017, *Remo Williams 2: The Adventure Continues* showed up, starring nobody that anyone's ever heard of but with the solid tagline of "A hero who doesn't exist must save America from another enemy we never knew we had."

Thinking about it, it's not too surprising that it didn't succeed, as fun as it clearly is, as it had little relevance to the time.

In 1985, Ronald Reagan had just been emphatically returned to office but this film hints at his *Star Wars* program being an expensive fake and his military as alternately inept and corrupt at the highest levels. Setting up American soldiers, if only a few of them, and the military industrial complex as the bad guys might sound obvious nowadays but it went well against the grain in patriotic 1985.

What's more, the characters we're supposed to root for are hardly what we expected at the time. Fred Ward does a solid job as Remo, but he isn't a musclebound giant; no other eighties action hero could have followed up an action movie like this with *The Prince of Pennsylvania*, in which he finds

himself kidnapped by his own son, played by Keanu Reeves. Maybe Fred Ward should have trained with Chiun as well.

Ah yes, Chiun! Him too. Beyond the fact that an Oscar-winner was cast in yellowface as late as 1985, he's likely to piss off most of the potential audience. Let's see now. He believes that "professional assassination is the highest form of public service". He's a racist who believes that anyone not born Korean has been hamstrung in life. And he's an unapologetic sexist who manages to shut up our gutsy major by telling her that, "Women should stay home and make babies. Preferably man child." Oh, and he uses some sort of Vulcan nerve pinch to quiet her tongue. "Bressed sirence," he mutters in his Japanese take on the Korean tongue and, after that, her promising part is worthless. In other news, Donald Trump has appointed Chiun as his new Secretary for Overseas Aid.

More than anything, I think audiences wanted firepower in 1985. They wanted their heroes to be incredibly well-armed with unlimited ammo to blow up everything in sight. You didn't watch Schwarzenegger movies for the vibrant acting or the realistic storylines, right? As Xander Cage wisely stated in *xXx*, "Dude, you have a bazooka. Stop thinking Prague Police and start thinking PlayStation. Blow shit up!" Now, *Remo Williams* does provide plenty of decent explosions, but Chiun teaches Remo to rely on his mind and body rather than any weapon. After all, what use is a gun when you can dodge bullets?

Personally, I adored his improvisational skills. There's a scene here with Remo and Major Fleming locked inside a gas chamber to die. How does he get them out? Well, he suckers in the gas masked nutjob responsible, beats him up, pulls off his mask and uses the gaudy diamond on his front tooth to scratch an X in the reinforced glass observation wall so that he can then dive through it. That's my sort of action, but apparently not that of most Americans in 1985. There are reasons why the film was only called *Remo Williams: Unarmed and Dangerous* abroad; it's objectively a much better title but unarmed is frankly un-American, right? I'm shocked that the N.R.A. didn't mount a boycott.

Even if audience members were willing to stay with such pinko liberal commie propaganda on the screen, they just didn't seem to buy into the wild talents of the *Destroyer* series, that extends beyond the martial art of Sinanju, whose name might even at the time have sounded ridiculous—the original children's book of *Jumanji* was first released in 1981—to a trio of dobermanns who can pull down ladders with their teeth and run up stairs.

Again, I personally love the fact that Chiun can dodge bullets, walk on water and be impervious to heat. I love that he knows the "twenty steps designed to bring a woman to sexual ecstasy" though he's "rarely found it necessary to go beyond seven to achieve bliss." I love that he has only one student but he puts him at constant risk of death, only occasionally feeling the need to step in and help out. But hey, I'm a *Doc Savage* fan more than a

Superman fan, so I always appreciate superpowers more when they're the result of dedication and hard work than when they're due to being bitten by a radioactive gnat or born on an alien planet with a magic sun. That's in other people, I should emphasise! I'm entirely open to being gifted a set of superpowers myself for doing precisely nothing. Please let me know if that's covered on my medical!

As wildly overdone, politically incorrect and abundantly convenient as this film is, I'm surprised *Remo Williams*, whatever its subtitle, hasn't found a more enthusiastic cult audience. It has all the component parts needed: huge explosions caused by laser weaponry, some death-defying stuntwork (which was often done by Fred Ward himself) and an underlying message of vigilante morality, delivered with an extra dose of testosterone.

How much testosterone, you might ask? Well, Remo doesn't just kill the big bad boss, he tosses him over a car that's leaking fuel, picks up a stick from the ground, rubs it with two fingers until it catches fire and then nonchalantly tosses it back to blow the bastard's ass up. He doesn't even look back to see the results! Yeah, even Arnie isn't that cool.

The Awesomely Awful '80s, Part 2

The Awesomely Awful '80s, Part 2

Crimewave

Director: Sam Raimi
Writers: Ethan Coen, Joel Coen and Sam Raimi
Stars: Louise Lasser, Paul L. Smith, Brion James, Sheree J. Wilson, Edward R. Pressman, Bruce Campbell and Reed Birney

If *Remo Williams: The Adventure Begins* was full of established talent, *Crimewave* was full of future talent that was at its most inventive at the time and that leaps out afresh every time I watch it.

It was directed by Sam Raimi, who had made a big splash on the indie circuit with *The Evil Dead*. He also wrote it, with a couple of brothers who had just made their own splash with their own indie feature called *Blood Simple*. They're Joel & Ethan Coen, who have an impressive array of Oscars between them now, for films like *Fargo* and *No Country for Old Men*. Sam Raimi doesn't have any of those but he did go on to some much bigger things, such as a fantastic pair of *Spider-Man* movies (the third only exists for me in that alternate universe where *The Phantom Menace* and *Indiana Jones and A Fridge Too Far* were made).

All those folks have explored film history throughout their careers and found ways to make it work afresh for them but, clearly invigorated by the success of their first respective features, they went overboard with that approach in their second, which, at heart, is really a Hitchcockian thriller where a mild-mannered nobody is unexpectedly caught up in the web of a dastardly and murderous plot. Think *North by Northwest*.

Now, Hitchcockian tension isn't what comes to mind when *Crimewave* kicks in; it only takes a couple of scenes to realise that we're also watching a sort of live action cartoon, with everything (and I do mean everything) deliberately overplayed. As an outright heel called Renaldo, for instance, Bruce Campbell doesn't merely blow smoke rings, he makes that smoke turn into naked dancing girls. When a bad guy is whacked with a frying pan, he falls against a wall hard enough for a shelf to tip and three large bowling balls roll down onto his head. This is *Looney Tunes* bedrock.

To many of you, the presence of Bruce Campbell is all you need to know but I'll add that the entire picture is a flashback told by a nerdy security guard about to be electrocuted for a murder he didn't commit. There's a car full of nuns chasing their way to the Hudsucker State Penitentiary to save him, crossing themselves all the way, but we hear his story first, just as Hitchcock would have told it. Well, not at all like Hitchcock would have told it, actually, unless there's an alternate universe version of *North by Northwest* that features Roger Rabbit rather than Roger Thornhill.

Let me set up the crime, because it's quintessential Coen Brothers. Over at Odegard-Trend Security Systems, Odegard is screwing Trend out of his half of the company but Trend has found out and called in Center City Exterminators for a hit (motto: "we kill all sizes"). So far, so noir, but we're about to meet those hitmen in their exterminator van that's so incognito it has a giant rat on its roof.

Paul L. Smith and Brion James are character actors you'll have seen in many movies without probably remembering their names. Smith was the Beast Rabban in *Dune*, Bluto in *Popeye* and Falkon in *Red Sonja*, though I know him best from this film and the outrageous *Sonny Boy*. James was

The Awesomely Awful '80s, Part 2

Leon in *Blade Runner*, Kehoe in the *48 Hrs* movies and Requin in *Tango & Cash*, but he was perhaps most memorable as the mass murderer Meat Cleaver Max in *The Horror Show* aka *House III* (covered later in this book).

As Faron and Arthur Coddish, wild and wacky exterminators, they're the closest thing I've ever seen to cartoon characters on legs. They have cartoon voices and cartoon actions and they channel the Three Stooges constantly. Oh and yes, they have a portable electrocution device, vaguely reminiscent of a proton pack, whose power is measured in "megahurts". In other words, to extend that alternate universe *North by Northwest*, it's like James Mason had hired the double act of Wile E. Coyote and Marvin the Martian to kill off Roger Rabbit.

Roger Rabbit (in the form of actor Reed Birney) is Vic Ajax, our nominal hero who's stereotypically nerdy enough to have a book called *How to Talk to Girls* in his pocket. He really needs it too, because he makes me look like I know how to talk to the ladies. He's our unreliable narrator, about to be executed for being in the wrong place at the wrong time because Trend gave him the evening off to find that special someone, rather than let him go back to the office and find Odegard's corpse.

"Of course, the perfect woman isn't just going to walk into my life," he mutters, as the perfect woman walks into his life from across the street.

The Awesomely Awful '80s, Part 2

And gets hit by a van. With a giant rat on its roof. Everything ties together in this film, which unfolds for the most part at a single junction in a single city, with Odegard-Trend Security Systems on one corner, the Rialto Club on another and the apartment block at which everyone lives on a third.

Incidentally, the production spent a week in Detroit shooting at night with their fictional storm generated by fans from the sort of airboats on which you take tours through Louisiana swamps. In his autobiography, *If Chins Could Kill*, Campbell remembers one scene underneath a retirement home which was interrupted by a bottle being thrown down to the street, with a note inside reading, "The noise is keeping me awake all night long and I am getting sick. I'm dying because of you."

Vic falls immediately in love with Nancy but she's with Renaldo, who's so outrageous that he steals every single scene. "I'm not that sort of girl," she tells him, over dinner at the Rialto. "Well, with a little practice," he tells her, "you could learn to be." He hurls zingers so fast that we literally hear them ricochet. "I haven't seen you here before," he tells another girl at the bar. "I like that in a woman." He tries it on with her later, in the street. "Hey, baby. Why don't you come over to my pad," he suggestively asks. "We'll have a scotch and sofa."

The bulk of the film follows the hitmen's ever-expanding attempts to

The Awesomely Awful '80s, Part 2

kill off witnesses. They take down Odegard easily enough, but accidentally add Trend to the tally too when he "investigates" what he believes is an empty crime scene. Then they go after Trend's wife, Helene, who's been watching from a high up window opposite. Then it's the apartment manager who interferes. Then it's Nancy. Then it's...

There's some fantastic filmmaking here, with real imagination in the scripting, the camerawork and the editing, not to mention the amazing tie between on screen action and a wild score. Of course, it's so madcap that it's impossible to categorise it. It cycles through being a film noir, then a romance, then a horror movie, then a thriller, then an action flick, then an inspirational Lifetime Channel movie of the week. Even as a comedy, it can't stay consistent; it's continually a black comedy, a live action cartoon and a riff on the Three Stooges and if you can't imagine a film that's all three at once, then this is surely going to be an eye opener for you!

What's most amazing is how the crew managed to make any of it work, given the crazed production, which included all sorts of bizarre problems and outrageous interference by Embassy Pictures, who had initially given Raimi full creative freedom but then interfered with everything before, during and after the shoot. Often, their reasoning was inexplicable.

For instance, Raimi wanted his old friend and frequent collaborator,

Bruce Campbell, for the lead role of Ajax, but Embassy refused because they wanted a "name actor" instead. That's understandable, I guess, but they chose to cast Reed Birney, who had only made two pictures in the previous decade, neither of them remotely the success that *The Evil Dead* had been. Campbell was relegated to a supporting slot which Raimi and the Coens then bulked up considerably. Birney does fine, but we can't fail to look back from the 21st century and wonder how different the film would have been with the Big Chin in the lead. Of course, who would then play Renaldo?

The experience was soul crushing for the young crew. Campbell vowed never to work with big budget producers again. Raimi called the post-production experience "a horrible, horrible, horrible, depressing scene." John Cameron, the second assistant director, said that, "if you survived that experience, nothing in the business could ever be as hard again."

How hard was it, you might ask? Well, Trend's wife, Helene, is played by Louise Lasser, who had been married to Woody Allen and played the lead on *Mary Hartman, Mary Hartman* for 325 episodes. Campbell details that she fired her make-up artist under the influence of cocaine and insisted on doing it all herself from then on. They let her do whatever she wanted, as clownish as it got, but then fixed it on set under the guise of touch-ups. He

also adds that Brion James, presumably also coked up, destroyed his hotel room because "the ghost of his girlfriend's ex-boyfriend was in the light fixtures". Trippy.

Yet, amongst all this chaos, which somewhat inevitably resulted in a fragmented feature, there's some true magic on the screen. I could easily conjure up a long list of personal favourites. There's the shot where Mr. Yarman miraculously survives being hurled out of a window from quite a few storeys up only to be promptly knocked down by the rat van, just as he thinks he's safe. Trust me, it's hilarious. There are the shots where Helene throws all her crockery at Faron Coddish and the camera follows them through the air like she threw that too. There's a shot where Faron pulls everything in the entire room towards him, furniture and all, simply by yanking on the carpet. There are a whole slew of them during the car chase scene through Detroit.

However, one of the most memorable scenes in all of eighties cinema is the chase through "the Parade of Protection", marked as "the safest hallway in the world". Helene Trend twirls through a collection of pastel coloured doors, elegantly closing them all behind her. Faron Coddish, in pursuit, simply crashes through every one. He's blocked by the final door, which is made of metal rather than wood, so has to attempt to escape back

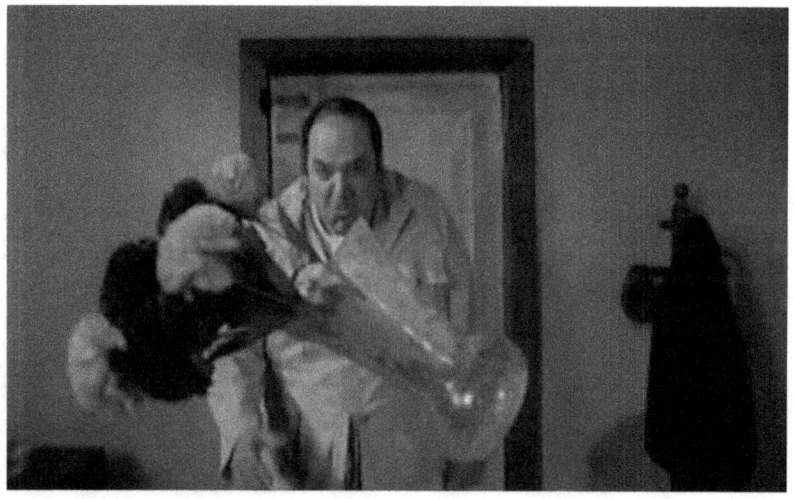

The Awesomely Awful '80s, Part 2

through the holes he's made when she pushes them all down on him like a giant set of dominoes. It's a scene that, today, brings to mind some of what the Coens later did in *The Big Lebowski*, but it felt utterly unique in 1985.

Anyone with an interest in any or all of Sam Raimi, the Coen Brothers, Bruce Campbell or a half dozen character actors should check this film out, but it'll be wilder than you think it is, even if you've just read this review. In 1985, it didn't help any of them. The film was a flop, considered unmarketable because of its constant genre-hopping. Campbell reports that Embassy only released it in Kansas and Alaska, to meet the minimum screening requirement for broadcast on HBO.

Frankly, I see the difficulty in categorising it as its biggest asset. It's no surprise that it's built up something of a cult following over the years. Do yourself a favour and join the cult.

The Awesomely Awful '80s, Part 2

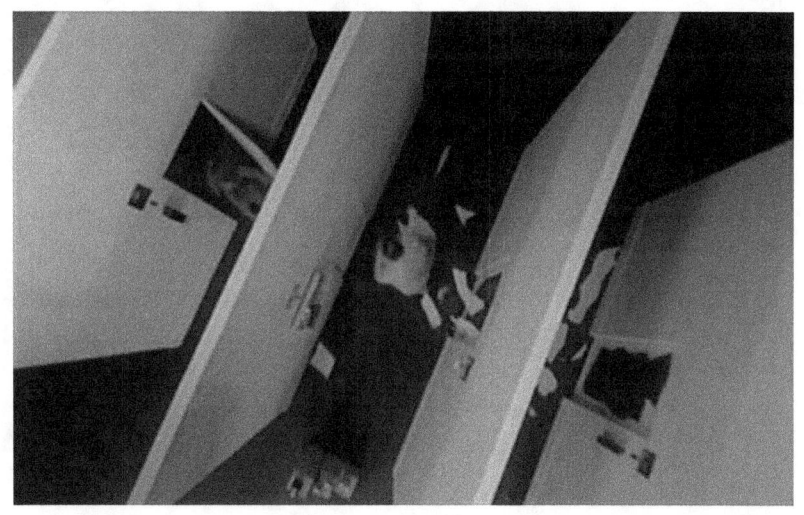

The Awesomely Awful '80s, Part 2

The Last Dragon

Director: Michael Schultz
Writer: Louis Venosta
Stars: Taimak, Julius J. Carry III, Chris Murney, Leo O'Brien, Faith Prince, Glen Eaton, Mike Starr, Jim Moody and Vanity

You usually know you're in trouble when the star of a movie only goes by one name, because you just know that it's because of rampaging ego and that's going to translate onto the screen. Well, with *The Last Dragon*, both the leads go by one name and we hadn't even heard of one of them until this film came out.

Vanity had some justification, at least, because Prince took her under his wing in 1982 and renamed her from D. D. Winters because he felt that she was his female incarnation. But who's Taimak? Well, nobody had a clue. He was just some nineteen year old non-actor who apparently knew some martial arts. How bad would he be as the lead of a major motion picture? In fact, never mind the non-acting, how bad is he going to be as an African American martial artist dubbed Bruce LeRoy in a movie whose full title is *Berry Gordy's The Last Dragon*?

Berry Gordy, if you don't recognise the name, was the founder of the Motown record label, a vastly important man but not a big name in the film industry and not someone you might expect to associate with kung fu flicks. Blaxploitation maybe, but his previous production credits were on music-related films like *Lady Sings the Blues*, with Diana Ross playing Billie Holiday, and *The Wiz*, the all-black musical version of *The Wizard of Oz*. However blaxploitation had faded out with the seventies and so had kung fu movies and even Bruceploitation. Bruce Lee was a dozen years dead at this point. People had moved on.

Well, this unlikely late combination turns out to be a heck of a lot of fun, even if that newcomer, Taimak, can't act his way out of a paper bag.

He does look good, though. He moves well. He's badass enough to kick the goddamn title off the screen during the opening credits! And his training routine involves his Asian master firing arrows at him while he works out. He's clearly The Man and his unnamed master even tells him so. "We have finished our journey together," he explains but Leroy Green, Jr.—luckily Bruce LeRoy is just a nickname, perhaps in part because he wears a rather recognisable yellow jumpsuit at the kung fu gym he runs—doesn't believe him. After all, he knows full well that, once he reaches the final level, he'll experience a sublime glow all over his body. Yes, we're still talking kung fu here, folks! Get your minds out of the gutter. Anyway, the glow hasn't happened to him yet, so he can't be a master.

Therefore, his master gives him a medallion he claims was owned by Bruce Lee and sends him in search of a new master called Sum Dum Goy. What's most amazing here is that Leroy has no idea that this is a joke. Really! Can you imagine wandering around New York City asking for Sum Dum Goy? I'm not even Jewish, but oy vey!

Fortunately, that search is promptly interrupted by a glorious scene in a bona fide 42nd Street grindhouse theatre (aka Heaven on Earth for fans of the awesomely awful). The screen is showing *Enter the Dragon* and Bruce Lee is about to fight big Robert Wall. Leroy is in the front row, eating popcorn with chopsticks (is that a thing?) and not taking off his coolie hat;

what sort of manners did his master teach him? The rest of the place is wild, with a characterful, multi-cultural audience of drag queens, assorted thugs and children. A Rastafarian is smoking something spectacular. A couple of street hoods start dancing to a boombox before another patron stomps on it, synchronised to Lee stomping on Wall on the screen. Tough guys visibly cringe at Bruce Lee's famous testicle kick. And then, just to seal the scene, in comes Sho'nuff.

Never mind Taimak and Vanity, I adore this picture because of Julius J. Carry III, who I'd previously enjoyed as Lord Bowler in Bruce Campbell's weird west TV show, *The Adventures of Brisco County, Jr.* His film debut was in Rudy Ray Moore's *Disco Godfather* in 1979 and he carries on here as if the blaxploitation era was still in full stride. Sho'nuff is the self-proclaimed Shogun of Harlem and the theatre even pauses the movie to allow for his flamboyant entrance, heralded by six outrageous goons of both sexes in just as outragous attire, a sort of cross between punks, Black Panthers and kamikaze pilots. He even has his own entrance spiel:

"Am I the meanest?" he asks.

"Sho'nuff!"

"Am I the prettiest?"

"Sho'nuff!"

"Am I the baddest mofo lowdown around this town?"

"Sho'nuff!"

Now, Sho'nuff towers over everyone else, given that Carry is 6' 5" tall and his hair adds a few more inches to that. He's also clad in a leopardskin cape and belt over a red and black martial arts gi. Just in case someone doesn't acknowledge his supremacy, he promptly takes on allcomers on the stage in front of the screen. Suddenly, we're not in 1985 any more, we're in 1975 and 42nd Street is the place to be.

The catch is that Sho'nuff is really just a two bit thug who just happens to be big enough to bully people with ease. While there's a whole subplot revolving around him calling out Bruce LeRoy to fight him—one of his goons points out that "that's the only guy that stands between Sho' and total supremacy"—but that's hardly the most interesting or least clichéd thing going on in the movie, even if it's spectacular every time it returns to the foreground. There are a couple of other subplots to focus on, both featuring Vanity.

One features her professional life, as introduced on Eddie Arkadian's surprisingly large TV for 1985: "Live from 7th Heaven, it's *Laura's Video Hotpix!*" 7th Heaven is a club and Laura Charles is a VJ there, introducing such authentic kung fu songs as DeBarge's *Rhythm of the Night*. Now, at this point, she's only just heard the name of Eddie Arkadian because a scarily young William H. Macy has asked her to play a videotape he's sent in of his

The Awesomely Awful '80s, Part 2

latest girlfriend's latest song but, when she refuses, Arkadian feels the need to escalate using all the cartoonish arts of intimidation, up to and including outright kidnapping, to force her into changing her mind.

Vanity is the exact opposite of Taimak. He can't act but he can perform incredibly well in his chosen field of kicking people's ass every time they don't actually call him out for a fight. She, however, acts really well, but her performances suck royally. We're supposed to laugh at Arkadian's protégé, Angela Viracco, who's an embarrassingly squeaky white pop diva in outfits so outrageous that even Phyllis Diller would feel overdressed in them but, frankly, I'd listen to her over Vanity's singing any day of the week. At least she's outrageous, which this film really calls for. Subtlety has precisely no place in *The Last Dragon* and Angela Viracco couldn't even spell subtle. During one song, presumably called *Test Drive*, she wears a collection of reflectors in her multi-coloured hair, a license plate on her butt that reads 'HOT4U' and actual headlights on her, well, headlights.

Here are some other examples, just in case you feel there must be some subtlety lurking in here somewhere when Vanity's offscreen. Arkadian has a giant fish tank in his HQ (evil lair, apartment, whatever it's supposed to be) and that giant fish tank has a giant invisible creature in it that devours giant chunks of meat like they're nothing. To feed it, he has a henchman who's a boxer, albeit not a good one; he's inevitably called Rock and he

The Awesomely Awful '80s, Part 2

was so bad they called him "the Great White Hopeless". Later, when he feels he needs better help, he puts out an open casting call for murderers; some Mongolian goatherd shows up in a sheepskin, literally barks at him and headbutts the desk into two pieces for emphasis.

No, subtlety is not what this movie is about, though sometimes the lack of it does make for some interesting cinema. For instance, Leroy actually finds Sum Dum Goy; it's a fortune cookie company and it's run by three Chinese guys who are stereotypically black. Yes, you read that right. This film actually addresses the issue of race by mixing up stereotypes. Here, it's the Asians who loaf around playing craps and failing to notice Leroy's disguise because all black guys look alike. My heart sank when they have him join in their craps game but he introduces hopscotch to the rules. Hey, even Leroy's dad runs a pizza restaurant (motto: "Just directa your feetza to Daddy Green's pizza").

Now, if you're paying attention, I promised two subplots with Vanity. I'm sure that you won't be shocked to find that the other one is a budding romance between Laura and Leroy. What's a little more surprising is that Leroy's brother is pissed at this, given that little Richie is far from legal age. He's played by the fourteen year old Leo O'Brien, who's a natural actor and a joy to watch; he certainly acts circles around Taimak. I should point out that their younger sister is played by Keshia Knight, without the

The Awesomely Awful '80s, Part 2

usual Pulliam (while her run on *The Cosby Show* began in 1984, I presume this film was shot before it).

Knight gets little to do here, but O'Brien gets a surprisingly decent role for a fourteen year old, including some fantastic lines, most of them sassy, including one favourite I'll certainly never get to quote in public without getting beaten up, calling his brother a "chocolate covered yellow peril"!

Then again, this film was wide open to the kids: there's a fantastic tiny fighter who takes down a bunch of full sized bad guys and it turns out to be a twelve year old Ernie Reyes, Jr., in his screen debut; he would also feature in *Red Sonja* in 1985 and, only a year later, get his own show on the Disney Channel, playing the Last Electric Knight in *Sidekicks*, opposite Gil Gerard. Reyes would go on to have careers as a kickboxer, a stuntman and an actor. It's great to see him kick ass and take names here at twelve!

In short, this is a heck of a lot of fun even though it really shouldn't be. It's utterly predictable, each one of those subplots wrapping up precisely as you expected the moment they were conjured into being. Wanna guess if Eddie Arkadian manages to get Angela onto Laura's show or not? How about the result of the inevitable Leroy vs. Sho'nuff fight? Or the romantic angle; how do you think that ends up? And will Leroy ever reach the final level and achieve the mastery of the glow? If you can't answer all of those questions before you even watch the film, then you need to watch more

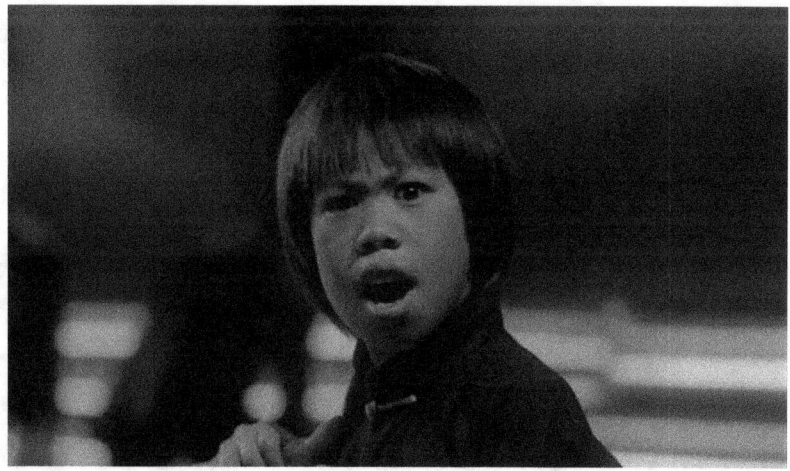

awesomely awful movies.

I'll end with a mention of the soundtrack, which surely has to be the only martial arts movie soundtrack to feature Smokey Robinson, Stevie Wonder and the Temptations. Sadly, it doesn't contain any of the songs by Angela Viracco, like *Dirty Books* and *Test Drive*. Actress Faith Prince was a real singer, though she specialised in musical theatre, where she won a Tony for the 1992 revival of *Guys and Dolls*. It takes real talent to be bad and still make it catchy which, come to think of it, really sums up the movie as a whole. Sho'nuff!

The Awesomely Awful '80s, Part 2

The Awesomely Awful '80s, Part 2

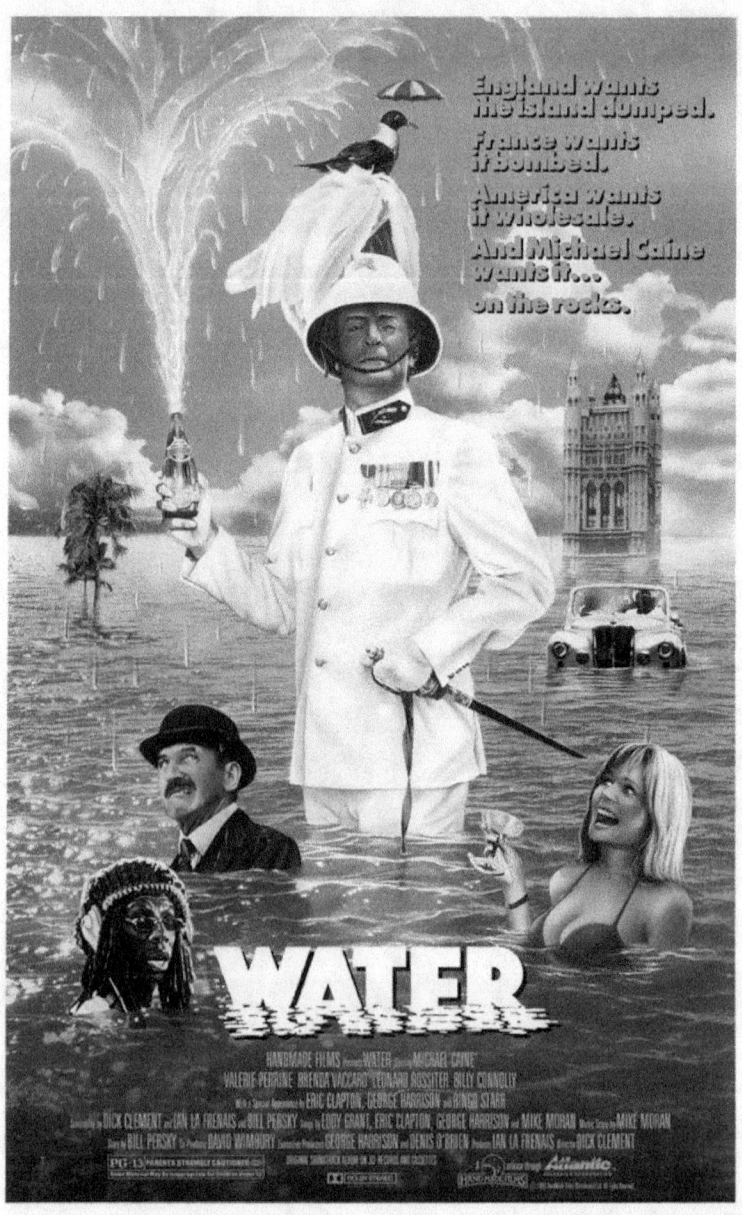

Water

Director: Dick Clement
Writer: Dick Clement, Ian La Frenais and Bill Persky, from a story by Bill Persky
Stars: Michael Caine, Valerie Perrine, Brenda Vaccaro, Leonard Rossiter, Billy Connolly, Dennis Dugan, Fulton Mackay, Jimmie Walker, Dick Shawn and Fred Gwynne

For all its martial arts, *The Last Dragon* simply couldn't be mistaken for the product of any country but the U.S.A. Similarly, for all that it's set in the Caribbean, *Water* simply couldn't be mistaken for the product of any country but the U.K. It's quintessentially British.

It was also rather topical at the time, framing a couple of recent events in a comedic setting. You see, we British have islands all over the place, relics of the colonial era, including most of those dotted throughout the Atlantic. Way down, almost to Antartica, are the Falkland Islands, which Argentina calls Las Malvinas; they seized them in 1982, sparking a brief war. Further north, just off the coast of Venezuela, is the Caribbean island of Grenada, which the Americans invaded in 1983 after a military coup. These events can't fail to translate into some seriously funny stuff, right?

Well, here, writers Dick Clement and Ian La Frenais, who had created a successful set of classic British sitcoms, including *The Likely Lads*, *Porridge* and *Auf, Wiedersehen, Pet*, took a story by Bill Persky, an American writer and director, and turned it into a riff on everything it means to be British, up to Maureen Lipman, playing prime minister Margaret Thatcher, citing Mahatma Gandhi in a call for action on the basis that, "One anorexic little loonie in a loincloth and we lost a whole subcontinent!"

The setting is Cascara, a fictional Caribbean island whose inhabitants descended from shipwreck victims (and the many "moments of weakness" of the local priest). It's a British possession but an ignored one. The last official visit was in 1898 and the aid provided after the Banana Blight of '79, the devastation of Hurricane Alice in '80 and the ensuing eruption of a volcano called Mount Pestilence amounted to bugger all. As the current governor, Baxter Thwaites, reports to his superiors in an official memo, "It would seem, in the eyes of the British government, that Cascara is the dot above the letter 'i' in the word 'shit'."

That governor is played by Michael Caine, who has a lot of fun here as a career diplomat who, through sheer inertia, has become one of the locals; ironically, he ends up fighting with them for independence. And those locals are a fun bunch indeed, as we quickly discover when the armed and dangerous Singing Rebel, played with zest by the then up and coming Scottish comedian Billy Connolly and who has "vowed never to speak until it's in a free Cascara", crashes through the roof of the local radio station to call for revolution in song.

"Throw off your chains and follow me," he sings, "and I will lead you to liberty." Of course, it doesn't work. As Jay Jay Johnston, the island's DJ, played by Jimmie Walker of "Dy-no-mite!" fame, promptly explains to his public: "Newsflash! In a daring raid earlier today, Delgado Fitzhugh and Garfield Cooper seized radio station Cascara and urged the people to take to the streets!" He briefly looks out of the window with binoculars, adding sardonically, "They didn't." The police arrive to arrest the rebels and he

The Awesomely Awful '80s, Part 2

keeps going: "They were later arrested and presented no problem. Hey, for the finest fresh fish in town, get down to Phil's."

What we soon find is that Cascara is a pretty rundown place—Thwaites won't send the Singing Rebels to jail for two reasons: he doesn't want to make martyrs out of them and it's still being decorated—but it has a laid back atmosphere that's truly contagious. The picture was shot on the real Caribbean island of Saint Lucia and I've wanted to visit ever since I first saw it here. I could blissfully live out the rest of my life spinning reggae records on Radio Cascara, playing dominoes at Aunt Matilda's Guest House and Domino Club and and writing books in my spare time.

Nobody else cares about Cascara, of course, at least during the set-up during the first third of the film. Sir Malcolm P. Leveridge, a career civil servant back in London, wants to evacuate the island and use it as a dump for nuclear waste, though that's mostly an excuse to finagle his secretary into a schoolgirl's outfit on a Caribbean holiday. He convinces the relevant minister, who hasn't even heard of the place and merely wants to be sure that the natives won't come over and drive his buses. The rebels want the Cubans to finance an uprising, but they don't care either. "Fidel says Cuba will shed blood for revolution of downtrodden peoples anywhere," they point out, "but you people are too downtrodden even for Cuba!" Tourism isn't an option either because it's a Caribbean island with no beach. The

local features, with delightful names like Desolation Bay, Point Peril and Calamity Cove, are hardly magnets for overseas interest.

However, one glorious accident sparks overseas interest in abundance. There's an oil facility on the island, which ran dry back in the fifties, but the company who ran it, Spenco, have come back to shoot a commercial, an entry into their "Hellholes of the World" series, featuring the fantastic Dick Shawn as insecure diva movie star spokesman, Deke Halliday. It's right after he throws the governor's wife Dolores over his shoulder, as he mistook her for the hooker he ordered, that they accidentally strike... not oil, but water. That's water with "a natural effervescence" and "a kind of tangy, lemony flavour". Some quick research later and Spenco realises that they've struck Perrier with an in-built laxative quality, appropriate as the real cascara plant, *rhamnus purshiana*, is a natural laxative.

Suddenly, of course, everyone cares about Cascara. Spenco immediately goes into the water business to wring every dollar out of the island it can. With big money on the horizon, the Cubans rethink Delgado's revolution. The British, realising that Sir Malcolm screwed up royally, decide to take action by having him quietly finance the same revolution in return for the bottling rights after they nationalise all local industries and kick out the Yanks. The Americans send in their military. So do the Brits. Even the French join in, on the grounds that Cascara has now become a threat to

their mineral water industry. And throughout, the world's news reports from the scene.

Standing in the way of all these foreign interests are a surprising set of rebels: not just Fitzhugh and Cooper, but Governor Thwaites too and an environmental activist by the name of Pamela Weintraub, who showed up to save the long eared horsehoe bat that calls the island home. That's an outdated relic of the British empire, a pair of Commie rebels and a pinko liberal environmentalist who's getting back at dad. Talk about engaging, sympathetic leads for the middle of the Reagan administration!

Water was an indie picture, made by HandMade Films, the production company co-founded by George Harrison in 1978 to finance *Monty Python's Life of Brian*. It subsequently brought us classics like *Time Bandits*, *The Long Good Friday* and *Withnail and I*. Harrison was generally hands off from their productions but took an interest here, most notably in the scene in which the Singing Rebels put their case to the United Nations, with a dream of a backing band that includes not only Harrison but Eric Clapton, Jon Lord, Ringo Starr and a host of others, poking fun at the Concert for Bangladesh, which Harrison also co-ran. As the TV director on duty cries, "It's Whosits and Whatsits together again!" Incidentally, that scene was shot in a single day and each of these legendary musicians was paid the minimum rate for a playback session.

I love *Water* for a lot of reasons, not just the glorious tone of Saint Lucia. I love the irreverent attitude, which is a British way of life. We don't like it when other people poke fun at us but we're happy to poke fun at ourselves all day long, especially our institutions, which means that so many British comedies are inherently self-deprecating. I guess that's inevitable with our history of walking into other countries and announcing to all and sundry that they're suddenly ours. I love the music, mostly by Eddy Grant but also featuring other musicians like Jimmy Helms, Lance Ellington and Mighty Gabby. I love the dialogue, which is inherently quotable, even more than I love the script which veers from surprisingly insightful to deliberately cheesy, like the brief conversation between Sandy "Take No Prisoners" Charlesworth of the S.A.S. and U.S. Army Major "Mad Dog" Hollister.

Perhaps more than anything, I love the casting choices. While almost everyone here is more famous for other work, in film, on television or on the stage, this is immediately what I think of when I see most of the rest of them elsewhere, with perhaps the sole exceptions of Michael Caine (for obvious reasons) and Fred Gwynne, whom I see as both Herman Munster and Franklin Spender, the larger than life Texan billionaire owner of Spenco who, when faced with blowing up his own daughter, mutters, "We were never that close."

Michael Caine is a neatly affable lead; he's so thoroughly down to earth that he's more interested in his experiments in crossing different strains of weed than in any official functions. Maybe that's why he's so relaxed, though he certainly displays a traditional British stiff upper lip and, in a rather unusual way, the responsibility of a colonial governor. "My job is a somewhat outdated institution," he points out, "rather like my marriage."

Dolores, his hilariously overwrought wife, who would do anything and anyone to leave Cascara, is played to glorious excess by the voluptuous Brenda Vaccaro. Thwaites jokes that, "Sometimes I think she misses the bright lights of Guatemala City." She spends much of the film in a variety of lingerie and nightgowns, bemoaning her lot in an outrageous Spanish accent. Needless to say, she's as unpopular with the locals as her husband is a hit and that leads to some hilarious reactions to her histrionics.

Fans of classic British film will see some similarities to a 1958 comedy, *Carlton-Browne of the F.O.*, which also involves a forgotten British island, a fight over mineral rights and an inept civil servant. The inept civil servant here, played by Leonard Rossiter in his last big screen role, channels some of what Terry-Thomas did as Carlton-Browne but it's such a quintessential Rossiter performance that we can't take anything away from him.

Billy Connolly was the first actor cast, because Denis O'Brien felt that he was the funniest man in Britain and, as Harrison's partner in HandMade

Films, was determined to cast him in everything he could. He's hilarious here but he's held back by his vow, at least until the Cubans set plastic explosives outside his prison cell and he can't think of a rhyme for bomb.

Others impress further down the ensemble cast. Dennis Dugan, as Rob Waring who's running the commercial at the oil site, is sharp. "We're with Spenco," he tells the Singing Rebel. "The ruthless yankee capitalists?" asks the Rebel's partner. "Of Houston, Texas," Waring snappily replies. Fulton Mackay is perfect as the lecherous local priest; many will know him as the prison officer in *Porridge* but others might remember him most as the lighthouse captain in the British version of *Fraggle Rock*. Valerie Perrine is suitably airheaded as Pamela Weintraub. Alfred Molina only gets one scene, but he shines while reading the menu for the dogs of war that the French have hired to blow up the Spenco installation.

HandMade Films really tried with *Water* but it didn't find the audience it wanted. It ended up a financial failure on original release and isn't edgy enough to have built up a subsequent cult following. As silly as it gets late on, it still feels right to me and I've often said that it's awesomely awful in my book. Well now it is, literally.

The Awesomely Awful '80s, Part 2

The Awesomely Awful '80s, Part 2

Gymkata

Director: Robert Clouse
Writers: Charles Robert Carner and Dan Tyler Moore
Stars: Kurt Thomas, Tetchie Agbayani, Richard Norton and Edward Bell

If Fred Ward wasn't really an appropriate action hero as Remo Williams, what were MGM thinking by casting gymnast Kurt Thomas?

Then again, they couldn't even figure out the genre from the outset. We start with a very ominous score, string heavy and reminiscent at points of the *Jaws* theme, but once there's more than just names for us to look at, it's Kurt Thomas doing a routine on the high bar intercut with shots of horses running. There are nine of the latter, carrying Richard Norton and a cool bunch of ninjas in pursuit of one man on foot. Is this action? Is it fantasy? Is it a thriller?

We'll find out later that the one man on foot is Col. Cabot, who is taking part in the Game, a cross between an endurance test, an obstacle course and a hunt. Any outsider who enters the imaginary country of Parmistan must attempt the Game. If they fail, they die. If they prove successful—and nobody has in 900 years—they get not only to live but to receive one wish from the Khan of Parmistan. Now, nobody getting into the country for nine centuries ought to mean that Parmistan is closed down tighter than North Korea, but somehow we're to believe that the Khan's right hand man, the warrior who shoots Col. Cabot, is Australian. Oh, and he's in league with the Russians. Consistency really isn't this film's strong suit.

Neither is establishing itself with credibility. Kurt Thomas, the man we saw on the high bar and are about to see on the parallel bars, was a real gymnast and a notably successful one: a Nissen Award winner, the first gymnast to win the James E. Sullivan Award for the best amateur athlete in the United States and a gold medallist at a couple of different World Championships who is very likely to have won Olympic gold too had the

U.S. not boycotted the Moscow Olympics in 1980. I looked him up on YouTube and his tumbling routines are truly insane. They actually had to ban some of his moves because they were too dangerous. In short, he's really, really good at what he does.

However, what he does is gymnastics and that really doesn't help his credibility in this action movie. Now, my grandfather was a gymnast who specialised in the rings, a discipline which requires massive strength and agility; he also served as a major in the Raiding Support Regiment, a special forces precursor to the S.A.S., so I know how tough gymnasts can be—but popular culture doesn't. Popular culture says that male gymnasts are wimpy gay wusses, one and all. It doesn't help that Thomas, who was 29 at the time, looked like he was maybe half that. He looks like he'd get beaten up by Jimmy, the Last Dragon's sassy fourteen year old brother.

So when Jonathan Cabot, the gymnast that this gymnast plays, gets recruited into the Special Intelligence Agency to enter Parmistan, play the Game, win it and then, for his wish, ask for the country to install an early warning satellite monitoring station just in case the Commies let their nuclear birds loose, we're more than a little confused. This kid doesn't even look old enough to drive, let alone drink; he has precisely no training as an agent; and Uncle Sam wants him to travel over to the Hindu Kush to do something that nobody's managed to do for twice as long as his home

country has even existed. Yeah, we can buy into that, right? We don't have any trouble with that. Of course not.

Well, no, even when he finds out that his father was an S.I.A. agent who tried the exact same thing but failed. I wonder who he could be! Yes, Col. Cabot was Jonathan Cabot's dad, so the magical power of movie revenge will apparently ensure his son's success. I haven't read Dan Tyler Moore's 1957 novel, *The Terrible Game*, on which Charles Robert Carner based his screenplay, but it surely can't be as ridiculous as this. And we're only ten minutes into the film thus far. Maybe it was based on a Mary Tyler Moore novel instead.

Now, to be fair, the S.I.A. are willing to let him train for two months to prepare, with Tadashi Yamashita and Sonny Barnes, but the point is really for him to invent an entirely new martial art, a bizarre mixture of karate and gymnastics, which I'm not sure anyone actually gets round to naming "gymkata" but which clearly provides the film's title. From the inevitable training montages, it apparently involves running, punching and walking up a spiral staircase on your hands. Oh, and producing both back and forward standing somersaults with a half twist. Suddenly, merely knowing the difference between a punch and a kick isn't enough for us to be able to interpret martial arts fights! I'm trying to figure out what a Thomas salto is and whether I just saw one.

Oh, and the other character we meet at this point is the S.I.A.'s own expert on the Game: Rubali, who's a stereotypically beautiful and deadly Parmistan princess. Whose mother was Indonesian. If nobody ever gets in, I guess insiders must get out of the country rather a lot, even though the journey can only be taken by pack mule and kayak. They don't even have a road, let alone an international airport with an overpriced power adaptor store and a Starbucks by every gate.

Anyway, training is completed and off go Cabot and Princess Rubali to Parmistan, via a salt mine in Karabal on the Caspian Sea (they say that a lot, just in case we forget the geography) to be supplied with cool gadgets because firearms aren't allowed within Parmistan. If you're to cheat, you might as well obey the rules while you do so, right? And these guys hunt human beings for sport but they don't like guns? That's weird.

Fortunately, there's a great deal to keep us occupied in the town of Karabal on the Caspian Sea. There's Col. John Mackle, a sort of low budget M, who dishes out low budget gadgets. There are a host of traitors who promptly kill off all the good guys and kidnap Princess Rubali. There's a terrorist training centre, led by a man with the worst movie accent I've ever heard; he looks like a midget Christopher Lee but he sounds like Tommy Wiseau! There's a big dude with a big scar across his face and a bigger axe in his hands, who thinks chopping a fire extinguisher is a

The Awesomely Awful '80s, Part 2

bright idea. There's even a frantic chase through the streets of whatever Yugoslavian city is substituting for Karabal on the Caspian Sea, with only one car. Yeah, that's trippy.

And, setting the stage for the rest of the film, wherever Cabot goes, his path is magically packed full of gymnastics equipment to leap onto so he can demonstrate his brand new martial art in a live environment. If you're being chased round an alley corner in Karabal on the Caspian Sea, just leap into the air and there will be a high bar stretching across the way for you to use in a gymnastics routine that involves kicking people very hard indeed while we're supposed to fail to notice that it's ready chalked for maximum grip. I can forgive this sort of thing a little, because Jackie Chan made a career out of it, but it shouldn't be this blatant and it shouldn't be prepared just for the opportunity. Just wait for the Village of the Damned, whose town square contains, get this, a pommel horse ready for kick-ass gymnastics action! To be fair, I'm exaggerating a little here, as Cabot does get to perform a lot of action scenes in places that don't have gymnastics equipment, but I'd love to know why the filmmakers ever thought they'd get by with that pommel horse of death!

Thus far, this has been relentlessly generic stuff, the sole element of originality being the gymnastics which, of course, is the most ridiculous of all. There's generic martial arts training, generic gunplay and generic Cold

War spy twists perpetrated by generic Cold War spies in generic raincoats, but there's nothing that really rips off anything in particular. That's about to change. Now, I have seen worse than this, but it's threadbare material, strung together and rendered laughable by a flamboyantly dynamic score, which would be great if only everything else could live up to it.

Once we get to Parmistan, we start in on the overt ripping off of films that we know. This is about to turn into *Enter the Dragon*, a rather more successful feature directed by this film's director, Robert Clouse. Then it'll turn back to *The Most Dangerous Game*, which it hinted at early on. Finally it'll turn into something rather akin to *Bedlam* crossed with *Westworld*, in which everyone in an entire town tries to kill Cabot while happening to be utterly batshit insane. How did this get pitched to MGM and why did they greenlight it?

We also get the truly bizarre experience that is the Khan of Parmistan, who surely realised how ridiculous his role was and so played it up for laughs. He's Buck Kartalian from Detroit, MI, the star of films like *Cool Hand Luke*, *Planet of the Apes* and *Myra Breckenridge*. Well, the star of *Please Don't Eat My Mother!* aka *Sexpot Swingers*, but he did play lesser roles in those bigger pictures, often memorably, as Julius was in *Planet of the Apes*. Here, however, he comes across like Mel Brooks with his vast moustache and lines like "Anyone trying to avoid an obstacle will be instantly killed!"

The Awesomely Awful '80s, Part 2

With that line, he was just outlining the scope of the Game here to a set of competitors: a three mile run to a swamp, a two hundred foot rope climb, half a mile more to the gorge, then into the river, on to the high forest, then the Village of the Damned and a five mile run through the swamp to get back to the city. "It's not all at great risk," he suggests with bright eyes before donning his Russian fur hat and wandering off with a grin to play king for his people.

Contrary to popular opinion, there are positive aspects to this film. I liked the Yugoslavian locations, even if I didn't like the constant depiction of the locals as inbred halfwits without teeth. The Kazakhs hated *Borat*; the Slavs would have hated this too, had it actually screened in their vicinity.

Some of what we see in the Village of the Damned is neatly freaky too, including a madman who has a face built onto the back of his head so that he can masquerade as a statue and attack you when you turn your back. There's a brief glimpse of a local sport in which ninjas on horseback try to enclose each other in nets. The fights aren't bad at all and this is an action movie with plenty of action. But the martial arts side is clearly set up to be *Enter the Dragon*, with Kurt Thomas playing Bruce Lee and Richard Norton as Bolo Yeung. Neither has a chance. Norton was responsible for the fight choreography, which is better than his acting, but this was early on for him; he'd fought Chuck Norris in *The Octagon* and played one of the title

characters in *Force: Five*, but the likes of Jackie Chan, Sammo Hung and Cynthia Rothrock were all firmly in his future.

Of course, there's plenty that's completely awful, starting with the whole idea behind the film. Parmistan is a joke and its Khan is beyond a joke. The Princess could have been used substantially but she's wasted in a routine romantic subplot. The rest of the story is idiotic and overblown, apparently trying to outdo its early inanities with worse ones later on. If the Game wasn't ridiculous enough to begin with, it's rendered worse by constant cheating and rulebreaking. Thorg is an outrageously ridiculous villain shoehorned into the second half of the film, Bob Schott looking like a drunk Matt Hardy. The wedding angle is stupid, as is the ending and the grand reveal that comes soon before it. The locations are good but the camerawork isn't and the acting is a disgrace.

Perhaps I can forgive Kurt Thomas, as he wasn't an actor, but nobody else. And I can't forgive his character; why does he stop and turn around every two steps when being chased, even halfway up a rope that's on fire? That got old quicker than Norton's embarrassing ponytail. So yeah, it's almost as awful as you've read that it was.

But hey, it's pretty awesome too because what other movie have you ever seen that mixes "the skill of gymnastics" with "the kill of karate"? Has

another movie even dared to attempt that? Should another movie ever dare to attempt it?

Well, to my thinking, the pommel horse of death must return! Now, all I have to do is do some research on fourteen year old male gymnasts, figure out where Karabal on the Caspian Sea really is and then convince MGM, who don't make movies any more, to make *Gymkata II*.

But hey, my American friends tell me that the moment you think about the Game, you've already lost. Sassinfrassin.

The Awesomely Awful '80s, Part 2

1986

Back to School
Howard the Duck
Maximum Overdrive
Solarbabies
Trick or Treat

The Awesomely Awful '80s, Part 2

Back to School

Director: Alan Metter
Writers: Rodney Dangerfield, Greg Fields and Dennis Snee
Stars: Rodney Dangerfield, Sally Kellerman, Burt Young, Keith Gordon, Robert Downey, Jr., William Zabka, Paxton Whitehead, Adrienne Barbeau, M. Emmet Walsh, Terry Farrell and Ned Beatty

Here's one of the best feelgood tonics I know. If the world is bringing me down—and one look at the news is likely to do that nowadays; don't you just pine for the good old days when the bad guys in movies were all Americans pretending to be Russians rather than Brits pretending to be Americans?—I just pop this in and, an hour and a half later, I'm laughing like a fool. Rodney Dangerfield was one of the great American comedians and his greatest talent was in one liners. Just look up any of the thirty-frickin'-five times that he appeared on *The Tonight Show* and sent Johnny Carson into uncontrollable laughter.

Or just see this picture. It's full of those one liners and what makes it work so well is that most of them hit and very few miss. "The football team at my high school, they were tough," he explains. "After they sacked the quarterback, they went after his family!" Or: "They asked a kid to prove the law of gravity, he threw the teacher out the window!"

Also, like *Water*, this is another movie with an all-star cast appearing in the roles in which I'll always picture them, even the star himself. Sure, he ran his own comedy club in New York for 35 years, one of the best venues in the business. Sure, he starred in *Caddyshack* and *Easy Money* and over a dozen other films. Sure, he even voiced a dog based on himself for the animated feature, *Rover Dangerfield*. I'll still always see him as Thornton Melon, the literally larger than life character that he plays here.

Melon is a rich and successful businessman, with 150 Tall & Fat stores to his name, selling clothes to those of unusual sizes. Naturally, he does so with one liners. Just check this ad out: "Are you a large person? Pleasantly plump? A little on the hefty side, perhaps? Well, let's face it: are you fat? When you go jogging, do you leave potholes? When you make love, do you have to give directions? At the zoo, do elephants throw you peanuts? Do you look at a menu and say, 'Okay'? Well, now you can eat all you want because, at Thornton Melon's Tall & Fat Stores, we've got you covered."

He's also happy with his life. Well, except for his second wife, Vanessa, played so viciously by Adrienne Barbeau that she seems like a completely different actress to the one I know from *The Fog*, *Escape from New York* and *Swamp Thing*. Here, she's an outrageous gold digger who hates Thornton and cheats on him any chance she can get. "We were doomed from the start," he later explains to a date, once times have notably changed. "I'm an earth sign. She's a water sign. Together we made mud." He comments to Lou, his chauffeur, masseur and hired muscle, that "she gives great headache."

Other than Vanessa, he's living the life he always wanted, but he can't forget the message that his father instilled in him when he was young and getting bad grades at school: "I don't care how rich or successful a man is. If he don't got an education, he got nothing." In fact, he remembers those words so well that he promptly ends up eating them, which shouldn't be at all surprising, given the context.

Visiting his only son, Jason, whom he thinks is doing great at Great Lakes University, he finds instead that he isn't on the diving team, he isn't in a fraternity and he wants to drop out of school. After all, *his* dad never went to college and look how *he* turned out. So, as ridiculous as it sounds, back to school goes Thornton Melon at the ripe young age of a heck of a lot to back up his point and there are two reasons why this works so well.

One is that it's extremely ridiculous. Rodney Dangerfield, who was 65 years old at the time, had never been seen in anything outside a joke. We had no idea that he even knew how to be serious; when he finally was, in *Natural Born Killers*, he was so serious that it truly scared us. Nobody can possibly watch this and see it as realistic in the slightest. We don't even have to get to his infamously impossible Triple Lindy dive, which would have killed him if he'd done it for real. Just Rodney Dangerfield in college is enough to make us laugh at the surreality.

The other reason is that, as surreal as he is, he represents reality in this film, as immediately highlighted by the fact that Dean Martin (that joke never gets old) doesn't believe that he's qualified to attend. Well, until he writes a big enough cheque that is, to found the Thornton Melon School of Business Administration.

This approach especially works in the business class where he argues with the professor, Dr. Philip Barbay, on his first day. "Oh, you left out a

whole bunch of stuff," he comments, after Barbay has them start building a company from the ground up with its own manufacturing plant. What it boils down to is that everyone needs their palm greased in the real world and that isn't anything that you're going to learn in college. You have to wait until you leave and that's where Melon comes in.

Of course, not all of it is experience; some of it is just street smarts and imagination. When term starts, which is conveniently right when Melon enrolls, signup for classes is a lot of long lines. So he has Lou stand out by the limo with a sign with Bruce Springsteen's name on it and suddenly the lines are short. This works well for a while, for everyone except Barbay. Even Phil's girlfriend, Dr. Diane Turner, who teaches literature, thinks that Thornton is just having fun. Then again, she's a free spirit indeed. Phil has a stick so far up his ass that he'd snap in half if he bent over.

Paxton Whitehead is perfect as Dr. Phil—that joke would have been in here too, if the show had been around at the time—so much so that I have difficulty imagining him any different, even though he's had a long career in both film and especially television, with long runs on shows like *Mad About You*. Diane is played by Sally Kellerman, who was Oscar-nominated for *M*A*S*H*, but I still see her as the flighty professor who lives her life in the moment and doesn't want to be merged or incorporated with stuck up Dr. Phil but just have fun.

The Awesomely Awful '80s, Part 2

The younger characters certainly have fun, except for Jason who finds himself increasingly alienated by his father's cynical approach to college. When his dad hosts "the greatest party in the history of the world" in a renovated dormroom, with no less a band than Oingo Boingo playing live, Jason sulks and walks out to be miserable all by himself.

Midterms are coming up and Jason's doing well, having finally found a spot on the diving team and finally spoken to the girl that he lusts after, Valerie Desmond. His father, on the other hand, is emphatically not. He has an upcoming paper on Kurt Vonnegut and he doesn't understand a word of it, so he hires Vonnegut himself to write it for him, prompting perhaps the single greatest cameo in the whole of the eighties, especially given the punchline that, "Whoever did write this doesn't know the first thing about Kurt Vonnegut!" He outsources everything to professionals, including his homework. "It's too light," he tells one such over-qualified substitute, literally weighing it in his hands. "It feels like a C. Bulk it up and add a few multi-coloured graphs."

Keith Gordon had already starred in *Christine* and *Dressed to Kill* and he was about to become a respected director, but he'll always be Jason Melon to me, the young man who tries hard to resent his dad but can't help but love him anyway, the student who just doesn't quite believe in himself enough to succeed, the rare example of a bullied movie kid that rings true

The Awesomely Awful '80s, Part 2

both while being bullied and while refusing to allow it any more. He's a lot of quintessential '80s characters, all wrapped up into one.

Similarly, Valerie Desmond is the sweetest unreachable love interest in eighties cinema. Sure, Terry Farrell went on to greater things and could easily spend the rest of her life at conventions signing 8x10s of *Star Trek: Deep Space Nine*'s Lt. Cmdr. Dax, but she's truly gorgeous here, soft spoken and a real delight. I'd be in line at one of those cons, but with a *Back to School* poster for her to sign. No wonder both Jason Melon and his friend, Derek Lutz, both want her really bad.

Oh yes, Derek Lutz. The actor who plays Derek Lutz with unique style has had quite the career since *Back to School*. You might know him best as Tony Stark, Sherlock Holmes or Charlie Chaplin, a role which deservedly landed him an Oscar nomination; he's never won but he has three Golden Globes and a shelf or two of other awards to his name. In 1986, though, Robert Downey, Jr. was a Brat Packer, in movies like *Weird Science* and *Less Than Zero*. He's very Brat Packish here too, with red and blue streaks in his hair and a hatred for society's norms. Lutz runs an anti-pep rally to piss off the school's American football team. Why? "We're pointing out that a violent ground acquisition game such as football is in fact a crypto-fascist metaphor for nuclear war." That's how I picture him. Screw Tony Stark! If I could afford a Robert Downey, Jr. autograph, which isn't ever likely to

happen, I'd be asking for his name to be on that *Back to School* poster right underneath Terry Farrell's.

The cast really doesn't quit. As Lou, Burt Young plays pretty much the same role he did in *Rocky* but with humour: "In his family, he's only the second generation that's standing up straight." Similarly, William Zabka, the professional asshole of the eighties and therefore probably the nicest guy in the world in real life, plays an over-privileged bully called Chas rather similarly to how he played an over-privileged bully called Johnny in *The Karate Kid*. M. Emmet Walsh is the quiet diving team coach who saw Melon dive on a pier in New Jersey, setting up what is still probably the most ridiculous movie finalé of all time, with Rodney Dangerfield's stunt double doing the Triple Lindy dive. Ned Beatty is an enjoyable pushover as Dean Martin. I've seen all of these actors before, some of them in dozens of movies, but I still picture them the way they are here.

A couple of other actors fit that description even more. Edie McClurg only gets about a minute of screen time as Marge Sweetwater, the private secretary Melon sends into Dr. Barbay's class to take notes for him, but she couldn't have moved a muscle better. And Sam Kinison is priceless as the contemporary American history teacher, Prof. Turguson. If you've ever seen him do stand up, you'll understand what Jason says about him. "He's really committed," he tells his dad. "In fact, I think he was."

What hooked me on *Back to School* were the jokes which are quotable in the extreme. I've used lines like, "Bring us a pitcher of beer every seven minutes until somebody passes out. And then bring one every ten minutes." No, I didn't use them with the flamboyant style that Rodney Dangerfield does here, but I used them nonetheless. That's the message of this movie, right? You can do anything that you want to do, especially if you have enough confidence to back it up. Why I didn't try to use, "What lovely girls! How would you like a life of luxury and deceit?" I really have no idea. I'd try it now but my wife would belt me and I don't want to lose her. She forgives my eccentricities.

What kept me coming back, though, was the truth that sits underneath the jokes and I don't just mean the cynicism that has college be, as Jason describes it, "something you do to pass the time until you go out into the real world and start buying people." I'm talking about how people don't read any more because, "Who has time? I see the movie. I'm in and out in two and a half hours." I'm talking about how Melon can't get a beer at a party in his own house but goes to get one anyway. And a sandwich, which horrifies everyone around him. "I hate small food," he mutters, hollowing out a entire loaf and emptying entire trays of food into it. I'm talking about how Robert Downey, Jr. can wear some frilly neckerchief under his overcoat and complain about the "bourgeois mentality of this school."

Now, not all these are good truths but they're truths nonetheless and I honestly believe that Thornton Melon's utter lack of embarrasment at any point in this picture and Derek Lutz's blissful lack of fear were formative influences on me. No, I'm not kidding. I'm quite serious. I've done a whole bucketload of things in my life that would have embarrassed most people, but Rodney and Robert and me, we know that that's perfectly OK.

I've got so used to liking fun films that flop rather than balloon budget blockbuster successes that I was rather surprised to find that this one was a hit. I had somehow got it into my head that people remembered Rodney Dangerfield for *Easy Money* a lot more than *Back to School*, but apparently I was dreaming. Made for just over $10m, this earned over $90m at the box office and added another $40m in rentals.

Today, of course, those numbers would surely prompt two entirely unnecessary sequels with increasingly horrific choices to replace Rodney Dangerfield and the sole consistent actor in the series being one of the bikini-clad girls under whom Melon goes scuba diving in the hot tub. M. Emmet Walsh would return to be the unlikely star of the third film, still playing the diving team coach, but Adrienne Barbeau would show up to play a completely different one, hoping that nobody would remember that she was even in the first film.

Fortunately, this was 1986 and successful movies were allowed to end when they should. The only sequel this needs is reality. If I ever decide to get a degree, I'll do it like Thornton Melon.

Howard the Duck

Director: Willard Huyck
Writers: Steve Gerber, Willard Huyck and Gloria Kats
Stars: Lea Thompson, Jeffrey Jones and Tim Robbins

Of all the films released in the awesomely awful decade of the eighties, one movie has garnered more hatred amongst movie fans than any other. Which one, you ask? Why, the very first Marvel feature ever released to theatres, *Howard the Duck*! There are levels of bad, you see, and way down there at the very bottom, below *Battlefield Earth* and *Highlander II*, below *Jack and Jill* and *It's Pat*, below even *Plan 9 from Outer Space* and *Manos: The Hands of Fate*, there's *Howard the Duck*, a movie so dire that nobody dares speak its name, a name more unspeakable than Hastur the Unspeakable.

Well, I beg to disagree. No, I'm not going to make George Lucas happy by suggesting that the tide has finally turned and that, decades later, the public is finally acknowledging it for the masterpiece he always believed it was. What the heck does he know? He made Greedo shoot first. He birthed the *Star Wars* prequel trilogy. He even bet Steven Spielberg, on the set of *Close Encounters of the Third Kind*, that it would clearly do better than *Star Wars*. He knows nothing! Well, OK, he knows how to sell plastic toys. He's pretty damn good at that. And he knows that *Howard the Duck* is better than its legacy would suggest. That's about it.

The film's biggest problem is simply that it doesn't know what it wants to be. It was based on a comic book for adults, written way back in the dark ages of 1973, over a decade before Alan Moore and Frank Miller made the idea of comic books for adults one that could be safely voiced in public without causing peals of laughter. There are adult scenes here, including one with Howard working at Hot Tub Fever, some sort of sauna brothel, that I never saw in England because it was presumably removed from the British release, probably because it was during the "won't someone please think of the children" era of movie censorship and everyone at the BBFC thought Howard the Duck was a kids' film.

But what would kids have thought of that scene anyway? Would they have understood it? I am very aware that the scenes that hint at a physical relationship between this lost space duck and Lea Thompson confused the crap out of a lot of kids back in the eighties. Was that hot? It certainly felt hot, given what Thompson wasn't wearing at the time! Or was it creepy? That's a frickin' duck, after all! Was this meant to be a gateway drug to waterfowl bestiality? Inquiring minds want to know.

I think adults found this childish, especially during the second half, and kids found it oddly adult, which meant that its audience was effectively reduced to the crazy folk who wrote it and George Lucas, who had stepped down as the president of Lucasfilm to make movies like this one. Willard Huyck, who directed Howard the Duck, and Gloria Katz, who co-wrote it, were friends of his from film school and they'd co-written American Graffiti with him, which was pretty good, so he assumed they might have a clue what to do with a wild idea like this one. Like I said, what does he know?

As the film begins, with smooth jazz and a cityscape over the water, so making us adults think this movie is an episode of Mickey Spillane's Mike Hammer, Howard is a working duck, returning from his gig in construction to throw his keys on the table and relax. What does it say on those keys?

The Awesomely Awful '80s, Part 2

"NO." And no, I'm not kidding. That's exactly what it says. Someone knew! Whatever story George spun them back in 1986 about masterpieces and ducks in brothels, they knew. They did have fun with Howard's apartment, though, in Marshington, DC. I particularly liked the poster for *My Little Chickadee*, starring Mae Nest and W. C. Fowls. What's that George Lucas poster on his wall? Ah yes, *Breeders of the Lost Stork*.

I especially liked the fact that his Earth is shaped like an egg, as we see when he's pulled forcibly off it, out of his apartment, through those of his close neighbours (oh hai, bathtub scene with duck boobs), up into space and through some magic passageway between galaxies that somehow allows him to continue to breathe, past the monolith that spits out the film's title, eventually dumping him down in a back alley in Cleveland, to be promptly kidnapped by a group of punks. This is, of course, incredibly realistic, as drug dealers and rapists were hiding behind every corner in the eighties, remember. That's why we had D.A.R.E. and ninja turtles.

Now, the punks pay no attention to the fact that this 2' 7" frickin' duck can speak, so literally throw him at some dork in a club as a joke date. Howard is then literally thrown back out by the bouncer who thinks he's a kid in costume. Because, you know, that's how you treat kids who try to sneak into clubs. You throw them out physically like they're Hollywood stuntmen who know how to not die on impact.

It's a hellish experience for poor Howard, of course, discovering that he's on the planet of the apes, a joke that's never brought up once, though the apes thing is brought up all the time. The only good thing to come out of the evening is that he meets Beverly Switzler, the gorgeous lead singer for the Cherry Bombs. She's a tough girl who can take care of herself, but somehow still needs our space duck to save her with his quack fu, because a couple of rapey fans decide they want to know her much better. This was the eighties, so it was her fault for wearing revealing clothing and walking a back alley on her own. Sometimes nostalgia isn't all it's made up to be.

Lea Thompson must have been seriously wondering about her career during these scenes. Sure, she'd like to forget her debut in *Jaws 3-D*, but she had made *Red Dawn* and *SpaceCamp* and she'd made a huge splash in *Back to the Future*. Shouldn't her career feel a little more promising than trying to identify the name of her planet to a talking duck? She takes him home to her decidedly non-punk apartment and, while he sleeps, goes through his wallet. She even takes out his condom. "What am I going to do with you, Ducky?" she asks. I have no idea if it's suggestive or not. Like I said, hot and creepy, all at the same time.

Just as we think we're watching a dubious porn movie with a slow start, everything gets childish, courtesy of the wild and wacky Tim Robbins. It would be almost two decades before he'd win an Oscar, for *Mystic River*,

but he might have won one sooner had his name not still been associated with this picture. He did direct *Dead Man Walking* in 1995, after all. Do you think the Academy really wanted to reward Mel Gibson for *Braveheart*, a picture which historian Peter Traquair accurately described as a "farcical representation" of "a wild and hairy highlander painted with woad (1,000 years too late) running amok in a tartan kilt (500 years too early)"?

Anyway, Tim Robbins plays Phil Blumburtt, museum lab assistant, like Harold Ramis played Egon Spengler in *Ghostbusters*. The man shouldn't be working. He shouldn't be allowed out in public without a chaperone. No wonder that one single meeting with him prompts Howard and Beverly to break up and go their own ways, at least until the space duck realises how tough a world we live in (and how tough it'll be for him, now that we're in duck shooting season) and they kiss and make up. Literally.

Philsy arrives on the scene just in time to see Beverly kiss howard goodnight in a very sexy silhouette. We've just watched the single most uncomfortable pre-sex scene in film history. She's in skimpy underwear. He's in the same bed. "Maybe it's not a man you should be looking for?" he hints. "Ah," she replies, "you think I might find happiness in the animal kingdom, Ducky?" Now, here's where that hot or creepy question is finally resolved. It's both, goddammit! It's not a coin we can flip. We'll wear our scars honestly.

The Awesomely Awful '80s, Part 2

Given that the plot here really just revolves around a duck showing up from outer space and wanting to go home, there's not much progression but what there is doesn't help. The first half, Philsy notwithstanding, is a lot of fun, even if it's the sort of fun that makes us want to take a shower afterwards. When Jeffrey Jones shows up, things go south, and that held true even in 1986, long before he got caught soliciting a fourteen year old boy to pose for nude photos. Watching after that happened makes this inappropriately sexy kids movie even more inappropriate.

Jones, who would do well in *Ferris Bueller's Day Off* and *Beetlejuice* and a bunch of other eighties must sees, does well here for a little while before the production metaphorically cuts his hamstrings. He plays Dr. Walter Jenning, an astrophysicist whose illicit experimentation at Dynatechnics turns out to be why Howard's here in the first place; it's something about bad alignment of his laser spectroscope or some such. Rather than wonder about how convenient it is that Philsy the nobody happens to know this bigshot astrophysicist (maybe all scientists hang out at the same Denny's), we realise that Dr. Jenning is Howard's ticket home. All he has to do is the exact reverse of what he did and we're golden.

Well, it doesn't quite go that well. The laser spectroscope malfunctions, explodes and pops one of the Dark Overlords of the Universe right into Jenning's body. You know, that sort of not quite that well. What this

means for the intrepid Jeffrey Jones, given that nobody on the picture had apparently heard of overdubbing, is that he has to stop all motion, start speaking in an annoying monotone growl and also spout lines that would sound unrealistic on a Saturday morning cartoon. You know when your six year old pretends to be a robot and ends up sounding like the Kurgan from *Highlander*? Just like that. But with worse dialogue. And with the pauses of a William Shatner and the grasp of metaphor of a Drax from *Guardians of the Galaxy*. Never mind that double bill of *Can't Stop the Music* and *Xanadu*, this part is surely why the Razzies were really invented.

How bad is it, you might ask? Oh, where do I start! "I'm not Jenning any more. The transformation is complete. I am now. Someone else." Imagine your six year old robot saying that. After a waitress at Joe Roma's Cajun Sushi asks him what's wrong with the specials, he replies, "This will mean the extinction. Of all existing lifeforms." Best of all, given that he's about to destroy our entire planet, he acts all coy. "I have disguised my true form. Which would be considered. Hideous and Revolting. Here."

And suddenly our children's film (with its occasional bundle of naked people getting it on in a love palace and its hints at interstellar bestiality) turns into a sci-fi/horror movie. Stunts. Wanton destruction. Convenient neutron disintegrators. A tentacle coming out out of Dr. Jenning's mouth. Monsters right out of the Cthulhu mythos, the big one reminding of an

unholy union beween a lobster, a scorpion and a Predator. All because Dr. Jenning accidentally freed one of the Dark Overlords of the Universe, who had been exiled eons ago to a region of demons, and said Dark Overlord now wants all his mates to come over for a party.

Oh, but yeah, it's a movie for kids. So Beverly gets to be the nicest punk rock chick ever, while half naked and chained under a laser spectrometer. Her reaction to her imminent sacrifice by a Dark Overlord of the Universe, who's just absorbed the power of a nuclear reactor and who spits acid? Oh, she shouts over to her duck lover: "Run, Howard. He's in a bad mood."

If you ever look up "guilty pleasure" in the dictionary, you shouldn't find any words, just a movie poster for *Howard the Duck*. This film really should be the definition, because the arbitrary rules of taste, as defined by the self-appointed gatekeepers of our pop culture, explain clearly to us that, if we admit that we like *Howard the Duck*, we should be locked away from society to protect the public from our subversive attitudes.

I'm firmly convinced that Howard only surfaced again recently so that parents can truthfully answer the inevitable "Who's Howard the Duck?" question from their children with, "Oh, he's owned by the Collector and he shows up briefly during the end credits of the *Guardians of the Galaxy* films." It allows them to pretend this one doesn't exist, never existed and who would have such bad taste as to even think that someone would

create such a celluloid abortion? Here's *Guardians of the Galaxy* again. Now, shut up and do your homework. It has a good soundtrack.

But, really, for all its many, many faults, I have to grudgingly point out that *Howard the Duck* is a surprisingly fun ride. In fact, it's better for adults than it is for kids, because we can happily watch Lea Thompson strip almost naked, possibly even guilt free, and then wriggle her seductive way across her bed to Howard. It's enough to make us start thinking about duck cosplay. Now, who in Phoenix can do a good '80s Lea Thompson?

Maximum Overdrive

Director: Stephen King
Writer: Stephen King, from his own short story, *Trucks*
Stars: Emilio Estevez, Pat Hingle, Laura Harrington, Yeardley Smith, Joh Short, Ellen McElduff, J. C. Quinn, Christopher Murney and Holter Graham

Maximum Overdrive was such an emphatic failure for director Stephen King, adapting his own story into a movie for the first time, that he's used it as a stock response ever since. Whenever someone asks why he's never directed again, he simply responds, "Just watch *Maximum Overdrive*."

Now, like *Howard the Duck*, it's really not that bad and King's direction really isn't that bad either. There's a lot of fun to be had here, even if it's not in the same league as justifiable classics like *Carrie*, *Stand by Me* and *The Shawshank Redemption*. To be fair, it's stuck way down in the little leagues, not even, frankly, up to the quality of *Children of the Corn* and that film only works today because of the *Family Guy* joke when Peter confused them with the boy band Hanson. It got a lot more watchable after that.

King has called *Maximum Overdrive* the worst adaptation of his work and there's a heck of a lot of that on screen to choose from, in part because he created a fantastic idea called the Dollar Baby. Any filmmaker who wants to adapt one of his short stories can do so, for the princely sum of a single dollar, albeit only on a non-commercial basis with all rights reserved. It works too; that's where Frank Darabont of *The Shawshank Redemption* and *The Green Mile* fame, started out. On the flipside of his idea factory, though, there's plenty bad here to choose from.

King has partly explained why in an interview. A line like, "I was coked out of my mind all through its production and I really didn't know what I was doing," really doesn't instil much confidence. Alice Cooper was drunk as a skunk for his first three LPs of the eighties; he calls them his "blackout albums" because he doesn't remember writing them, recording them or even touring them, but then we don't listen to them for a reason. This is ostensibly more recognisable as the work of its creator.

King sharing his trailer with a mountain of coke, though, did have one serious effect that I shouldn't joke about: a radio-controlled lawnmower ran out of control and hit a camera support; the ensuing flying splinters of wood cost the director of photography, Armando Nannuzzi, one of his eyes and, subsequently, the production a heck of a lot of money (the $18m lawsuit was settled out of court).

As tasteless as it is to suggest it, that real life accident would have fit in wonderfully in the film itself, which is a sci-fi/horror flick full of death and dismemberment caused by machines. Why, you ask? Well, King would have us believe that a passing comet, draping us in its luminous green tail for eight days, has a rather bizarre side effect, that of bringing machines to life and turning them into homicidal maniacs who lust after human lives. You know, that realistic old chestnut. Just say no, kids.

Oddly, while you might think that originality might be the one thing this film has to its credit, that's not strictly true. Theodore Sturgeon wrote *Killdozer!*, a short story with a startlingly similar theme, for *Astounding*, as far back as 1944 and that was adapted into both a TV movie and a comic book in 1974, the title entering the pop culture dictionary in the process, so it ought to be fair to assume that neither this nor the 1978 short story on which it was based constitute the pinnacle of King's imaginative output and perhaps not even the pinnacle of King's imaginative output while strung out on cocaine.

The Awesomely Awful '80s, Part 2

To his credit, it does start well, with mild mannered machines growing, well, a little rude; King himself cameos as someone using an ATM which promptly calls him an asshole. Then there's the reason that many of us cared about this film in 1986, the soundtrack by AC/DC, King's favourite band. Most of their music that's used here wasn't new but it was great and it's fascinating to hear songs that we know by heart sound different when deconstructed and reconstructed in order to fit a particular scene. There's also a fantastic truck with a big fibreglass clown mounted on the front. It's for Happy Toyz ("Here comes another load of joy") and it's what some people, like my better half, find that they remember most about this film. *Maximum Overdrive?* Is that the one with the clown truck? PS: it's really the Green Goblin, even though it looks nothing like Willem Dafoe.

Gradually we focus in on the Dixie Boy Truck Stop outside Wilmington, NC—we can tell how high King was at the time merely by noting that we're not in Maine—which was a set built for the film so realistically that real truckers actually stopped there by mistake. The cast of characters are partly people who work at the Dixie Boy, for an asshole of a boss called Bubba Hendershot—he's running a scam where he hires paroled convicts and has them work nine hour shifts for eight hours pay—partly customers who were already there when the comet's effects took hold and partly other folk who merely find their way there because, I dunno, maybe they want to be part of the ongoing nightmare. I couldn't find a single valid reason for anyone except the kid, Deke Keller, who's trying to reach his dad who works there. He made sense, at least. Why would anyone else

deliberately try to run the giant gauntlet of homicidal trucks circling the truck stop like Injuns in an old western? They needed to pee that badly?

We've already seen how much damage these machines can and are very willing to cause by watching a bridge open with vehicles still on it. That prompts a wildly gratuitous dance of slo-mo collisions and plummeting watermelons. That aperitif goes on for what seems like half an hour before we move on to watch the ten wheelers driving up to the truck stop and settling in for the main course. Ours and theirs both.

In between, King muses on his idea and has us wonder what counts as a machine. Sure, the trucks that we see on the highway every day can weigh 20,000 pounds on their own, plus another 10,000 for the trailer and 50,000 more in cargo. Giving them life and homicidal tendencies at the same time makes them seriously dangerous weapons and they're the overt villains in *Maximum Overdrive*. But Wanda June finds herself carved in the Dixie Boy kitchen by an electric knife, sprinklers try—and fail—to act ominous and a little league coach gets taken down powerfully by a soda machine. So does his team, with one of them squished by a steamroller in a spectacular shot that we don't see because the censors required it to be cut—he wanted the blood pack placed by the body to be smeared on the steamroller and the grass, over and over, but it exploded instead like an outtake from *Scanners*.

One other imaginative approach is to find a positive side to machines coming to life. One young gentleman finds himself stuck in the Dixie Boy arcade where the vending machines dump out their stock and the change machine issues free money. Sure, they then hypnotise and electrocute him

but there's always a catch. Can't we just sit back and enjoy the apocalypse once in a while? You know, like in *Dawn of the Dead*? Well, not this time.

The cast is interesting, but not particularly well known, especially at the time. The only real star was Emilio Estevez, who was riding high after *The Breakfast Club* and *St. Elmo's Fire*, with *Repo Man* right before them. He's Bill Robinson, one of the ex-convicts working at the Dixie Boy as a cook. I appreciated the often unusual characters for 1986: not just Bill the crook turned cook but the pervert bible salesman—there are Chick tracts all over his car but his hands are all over his hitch-hiker—and the black driver of the Green Goblin truck. Bill, for all his past mistakes, does have a strong moral grounding that his boss will clearly never have and Estevez can do that flawed hero act in his sleep.

The most recognisable actor today is one of the newlyweds whose car is mysteriously unaffected by the comet. Sure, every other vehicle in North Carolina is trying to kill every human being it can, from the lawnmowers to the ice cream trucks, but their car is happily still on their side. Why? I guess it just had to be or they'd have never got to the Dixie Boy to take part in the film; they'd have been stuck walking to the Plot Conveniences R Us corner store instead for the inevitable Asylum mockbuster version.

Anyway, Connie, of the cute couple called Connie and Curt, is played to screeching perfection by Yeardley Smith, an actress who you might not know by name or sight but would recognise the moment you heard her voice. Only a year after this film, she'd land the role that made her famous, as the voice of Lisa Simpson. Now you can hear her, right?

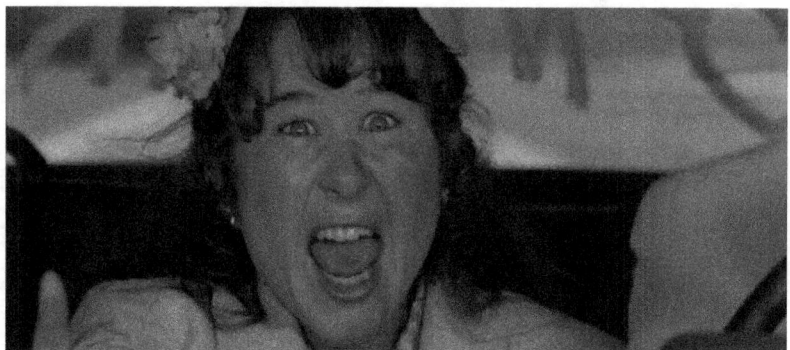

Oddly, it's not Yeardley Smith but Laura Harrington who utters the line, "Eat my shorts!" here, some years before Lisa's brother introduced it to the world on *The Simpsons*. This isn't the first use, Judd Nelson speaking it in *The Breakfast Club* too, but it's still odd to hear a line forever tied to one character spoken by another in an earlier film. It's like discovering that "Snakes. Why did it have to be snakes?" was first delivered by Daffy Duck. No it wasn't, by the way, so apologies for getting that stuck in your head, but wouldn't that be a riot? It's just as weird hearing Lisa Simpson swear like a sailor. And that does happen here!

Harrington is Brett Graham, Bill's love interest, who starts off strong and is then apparently entirely forgotten by the coked up Stephen King, just like most of the rest of the cast, which includes a whole bunch of good actors that neither you nor I have heard of. Pat Hingle is the only other name we might know, given that he played Commissioner Gordon in four Batman movies, but we really have no idea if he's good here or not as he keeps a cigar so tightly in his mouth that he mumbles like the Godfather after having a dozen teeth removed. Let's just say he has dialogue, even if he may well have delivered it in Swahili.

King is clearly more interested in the trucks and, rather appropriately given that his fiction is so full of brand names that an English friend once asked me to bring him back a Slim Jim from an American trip just because everyone in Stephen King novels ate them but he had no frickin' clue what they were, he lingers his camera longingly on their trailers as if it'll brand the names on our brains. The Miller Brewing Company must surely have

funded the entire movie based on how often we see that name and, while I have no idea what Thurston is, I keep asking grocery stores for it, along with Bic lighters, Mayfresh toilet paper and six packs of Laura Harrington.

What King always did best in his fiction is develop characters, especially young ones, but he gets precious little chance here with a large ensemble cast who occasionally get back in shot after another glimpse at the circling diesels. Sometimes I wonder if they blew up trucks with the bazookas that Hendershot conveniently keeps in the basement because they wanted to get another scene rather than to progress the plot or generate another big explosion to distract from it.

But those explosions do keep on coming and they keep us interested all the way until King remembers that he has human characters and decides to give them something to do, like pump gas for the trucks that manage to communicate via Morse code that they want fuel. And really that's what we have here: a string of explosions that punctuate the discovery of little character traits, while we wait for the trucks to quit stalling and just drive through the frickin' truck stop. Sure, we can play the armchair critic and consider this like *Cujo* meets *Duel*, but King has a point when he calls this "a moron movie". *Back to School* and *Howard the Duck* were both far more believable and grounded in reality than *Maximum Overdrive*.

Where King deserves some credit is in the way this film was shot. There are some truly powerful scenes here, both with and without human beings in them. There's one shot that would have functioned perfectly well as a still photograph: it features a school bus with a plane in it, vertically, as if it had fallen out of the sky like a giant lawn dart and landed right on top of the kids. It has precisely nothing to do with our story and it's gone quickly but it's a fantastic image that does more to convey the horror of a world where machines run rampant than almost anything else in the film. It's also the sort of shot that I doubt would ever exist without someone like Stephen King being involved.

Sure, this is a moron movie, with so many plotholes that the script must look like Swiss cheese, but it's also a blast to watch. Especially with friends and a case of Miller. And some Bic lighters. And whatever Thurston is.

Solarbabies

Director: Alan Johnson
Writers: Walon Green and Douglas Anthony Metrov
Stars: Richard Jordan, Jami Gertz, Jason Patric, Lukas Haas, James Le Gros, Claude Brooks, Peter DeLuise, Peter Kowanko, Adrian Pasdar, Sarah Douglas and Charles Durning

Hollywood movies don't just happen. There's a long and tedious process that goes through many people, often over many years, but it boils down to someone important enough liking an idea enough that he (and, yes, it's always a he) greenlights it and then the process shifts from "Can we?" to "How do we?" Often it happens because someone came up with a fantastic elevator pitch, a one sentence reason why that idea is awesome. As we saw with *Howard the Duck*, sometimes we can't help but wonder with the benefit of hindsight just who the heck greenlighted a movie and what its elevator pitch must have been for them to do so. Who thought it was a bright idea and why were they convinced? Maybe, like Stephen King with *Maximum Overdrive*, they were strung out on coke at the time.

Well, *Howard the Duck* was far from the only eighties movie that makes us scratch our head and wonder. *Solarbabies* is another, especially given that its elevator pitch must have been something like, "It's *Mad Max*, but on rollerskates." Who would greenlight such a picture? Well, Mel Brooks, that's who, he of *Blazing Saddles* and *Young Frankenstein* fame. Beyond the well known comedies he's directed, his production company, Brooksfilms, has made some surprising dramatic pictures, like *The Elephant Man*, *The Fly* and *84 Charing Cross Road*. Oh yeah, and this one.

He explained the process in detail to Blake Harris of the *How Did This Get Made?* podcast, but it boils down to trust and diligence and, in 1986, Brooks had too much of the former and too little of the latter. The modest $5m budget ballooned to $23m and, to get it completed, he had to put a second mortgage on his house. In the end, says Brooks, it did break even, but only with the new outlets that opened up over a quarter of a century: DVD and streaming and the like. He did learn his lesson, though and imparted that wisdom to the masses in his remake of The Producers in the form of Max Bialystock's two cardinal rules of producing: "One: Never put your own money in the show." And two? "Never put your own money in the show!"

Now, given that Brooks absolutely put his own money into this show, what did he get for it? That's a good question. "I'd say that about 65% of it is a really good, interesting picture," he suggests, "and the other 35%, you know, you can get through." He's got a point, even if we can argue about percentages. Let's see what you think. Picture this...

We're in the year 41 (which is in the future where the dates have been renumbered, rather than in some bizarre alternate past) and there's been some sort of calamity that has left our planet with precious little water: no oceans, no rivers, just carefully guarded supplies behind dams which are rationed out by the powerful Eco Protectorate. Our narrator is the warden of Orphanage 33, one of many bordering the wasteland, who indoctrinates his orphans to serve the System, even though he doesn't want to.

OK, that's cool, I guess. It's a dystopian future with an environmental angle. Sure, none of this makes sense yet, but maybe it'll get there. Hang on, what's that? Rollerskates? Why is someone rollerskating through the apocalypse? This isn't a zero budget, straight to video piece of insanity from Donald G. Jackson, this is a major movie, distributed by MGM and full

of people we recognise. But they're all rollerskating. With lacrosse sticks. Oh, and some long-haired dude skated up a crane and an owl flew down to land on his arm. What is this? *Rollerball* for kids? And who's this official who shows up to take them all in for perimeter violations, with his laser weapons and futuristic vehicles? He looks like either a performer from a New York gay club or a member of Judas Priest.

OK, let's take stock. Over at the orphanage, which is more like a prison where the kids break rocks for a water allowance, there's a skateball team called the Solarbabies. They're the good guys: Jason, Terra, Rabbit, Tug, Metron and little deaf Daniel, who's presumably their mascot. They were challenged by the Scorpions, who are the protégés of the big bad boss, Grock by name, who's someone big in the E-Police, to a game in the arena beyond the perimeter. Why? Because out there, there are no rules, so they can cheat. Oh, and Gavial, the bully in the Scorpions, serves as both the nemesis of the Solarbabies and a suck up to Grock, like a sort of one man Hitler Youth. In fact, that analogy works really well. Grock is the sadistic Gestapo leader and the Warden is the good Nazi, the one who got caught up in it all and doesn't know how to get out.

By the way, I provided names there because the film can't be bothered. While it's easy to figure out who's on which side, it takes quite a while for the faces to acquire names. How this was written by an Oscar, Emmy and BAFTA award-winning filmmaker, Walon Green, I have no idea. Well, OK, it's because the real driving force behind the script was Douglas Anthony

Metrov, whose biggest claim to fame at the time was that *Driller Killer* was shot in his loft. His goal was apparently to create the "Little Rascals of the future." In case you're wondering, he failed.

Anyway, now that we understand what's going on, let me shake that up a little. Grock breaks up the skateball game and the Solarbabies all run for the caves which, like everywhere in this post-apocalyptic world, are skate friendly. And there, in a puddle of water, Daniel finds a glowing orb that magically cures his deafness; he won't need electric ears any more, which is rather fortunate given that he literally just broke them. The first thing he hears is water dripping off the stalactites, which is prophetic, and the next is the telepathic communication of the orb.

Now, I'm sure you're wondering why. To any of this. And I really can't help. I have no frickin' clue. None of this makes any sense at all because nobody ever explains it. I can only assume that the priorities in this future dystopia are a little messed up. Water is life but keeping the places nobody is allowed to go safe for rollerskaters is apparently even more important. We don't even know why all the water's gone, let alone why some magic luminous volleyball can be the secret to bringing it all back.

The closest we get to an answer has to be the ball's names. Yes, names, plural, neither of which is Wilson.

It tells Daniel that its name is Bodhi. And bodhi is the Buddhist concept of enlightenment, the understanding of the true nature of things. Now, I'm no Buddhist but Wikipedia, that go to fountain for wisdom on religious

interpretation, tells me that bodhi "is knowledge of the causal mechanism by which beings incarnate into material form." Which kind of makes sense when you think about how this Bodhi makes it rain indoors. Then again, Wikipedia also says that the bodhi in *Solarbabies* is spelled "bodhai", which means absolutely nothing, so who knows. Maybe Metrov is a Buddhist who simply can't spell for toffee.

Later, after a set of unlikely adventures places the ball into the hands of Grock, he calls it the "Sphere of Longinus", which is surely a pun on the Spear of Longinus, the spear with which roman centurion John Wayne pierced the side of Jesus in *The Greatest Story Ever Told*, while he hung on the cross. Jesus, that is, not John Wayne. It's also known as the Spear of Destiny by those who credit it with occult power, people like Adolf Hitler, who, according to Trevor Ravenscroft's book on the subject, only started World War II so that he could capture it; taking over the world, creating a thousand year reich and exterminating the Jews were apparently bonuses only. Oh, and losing the spear results in death, which is clearly why Hitler committed suicide and General George S. Patton died in a car wreck in an army camp. Maybe reality is stranger than fiction even when fiction is as strange as this. Then again, maybe not.

Putting the two together, I still have no idea what this means. God so loved the world that he sent his only begotten son in the form of a cosmic bowling ball to teach the ways of the Buddha? I think it's more likely that Metrov was smoking something serious in 1986.

If he was, at least his trip took him and us to some interesting places. The owl boy from the beginning, Darstar by name, steals Bodhi, with entirely good intentions, and takes it to the Chicani tribe, to which he has no idea he belongs, who live in an abandoned wax museum, to which he's never been. Why? I have no idea. After that, the skate friendly road takes the Solarbabies to Tiretown, a wastelander carnival with an industry built around burning tyres. Why? I have no idea. Eventually, we find ourselves at the aquabunker, which is the dam run by Sarah Douglas from *Superman II*, where she uses a torture robot that's programmed to enjoy itself. Yes, I know. Why? I have no idea. But hey, it all feels cool, right?

At least this production, entirely shot in Spain, meant a holiday abroad for the young folk who populate most of the cast. You'll recognise almost all of the Solarbabies, I'm sure, even if Jason Patric was making his debut here, only a little less moody as Jason than he was as Michael in *The Lost Boys*. Jami Gertz, playing Terra, was in *The Lost Boys* as well, on top of *Sixteen Candles* and *Less Than Zero*. Metron is James Le Gros, from *Phantasm II* and *Drugstore Cowboy*. Peter DeLuise from TV's *21 Jump Street* plays Tug. Claude Brooks, as Rabbit, was best known for *Homeroom*, also on television. Daniel is ten year Lukas Haas, with *Witness* already behind him.

I should add that every single one of these capable actors is still busily working today with strong and vibrant careers one and all, but every one of them could have died the day the nineties began and you'd know them from all the same things. The same goes for most of the rest of the cast

too. Adrian Pasdar, from *Top Gun* and *Near Dark*, plays Darstar; not one of the Solarbabies, but allied with them as both orphan and escapee. Even the adults play along. Richard Jordan, as Grock, was Dirk Pitt in *Raise the Titanic!* and he also co-starred in *Dune* and *The Secret of My Success*. Sarah Douglas I've mentioned. There's even Alexei Sayle, who Brits will know from *The Young Ones* and Americans from *Indiana Jones and the Last Crusade*. Only Charles Durning, playing the Warden, really escaped the eighties tag, having been just as notable before it and after it.

Never mind that 65%, Mel Brooks. I'd say that 6.5% of it is a really good, interesting picture, but the rest is at least imaginative. Even when this is ripping off other movies, *Mad Max: Beyond Thunderdome* chief among them, it does so in an imaginative way. Max Rockatansky never used roller derby moves in order to leap over a collapsed bridge and he never pole vaulted over a security fence on rollerskates. Then again, he wasn't appearing in a picture whose $18m budget overrun surely went entirely on transforming the post-apocalyptic landscape of Almería, most frequently remembered for its spaghetti westerns, into a gigantic skate park. He could have just shown up inside a souped-up muscle car with spikes and gone anywhere. That budget could been allocated instead to figuring out an answer to the couple of dozen questions why.

Then again, maybe this works best when we don't have a clue and we just go with the flow, man. Unless, of course, that's a wildly inappropriate comment for a world without water.

The Awesomely Awful '80s, Part 2

Trick or Treat

Director: Charles Martin Smith
Writers: Rhet Topham, Michael S. Murphey and Joel Soisson
Stars: Marc Price, Tony Fields, Lisa Orgolini, Doug Savant, Elaine Joyce, Gene Simmons and Ozzy Osbourne

Ah yes, *Trick or Treat*. Not *Trick 'r Treat*, the much later horror anthology of note, but *Trick or Treat*, one of my personal favourite guilty pleasures from the awesomely awful eighties. I remember it well. Except, watching afresh, I was rather shocked to discover that it's not such a guilty pleasure any more. It's not that the film has got better, it's just got more relevant and it has a dark edge to it now that it never had when it was released. But more on that later. Why do I remember it so fondly?

Well, in 1986, I was fifteen years old and I'd just discovered heavy metal. I was two years into a glorious voyage of discovery that became my life for a decade and is still important to me today. The catch was that, while we Brits had invented the genre, it was an underground monster in the UK in the '80s and I wasn't yet old enough to be able to tap into it properly. My gigging years were in the future because my parents, never big music fans, had been given the impression that metal concerts were dangerous and so wouldn't let me go to any. Don't worry, I made up for lost time later!

I looked up to Eddie Weinbauer, the lead character in this film, because he was ahead of me. Just look at all those posters in his room and that long shelf of albums! He clearly had much more money than I did, even though I was running a newspaper round, and he even had a car, so he could go places a lot easier than I could on a mountain bike. Like WZLP, a radio station that played metal, courtesy of a DJ called Nuke, with whom Eddie is on a first name basis. Nuke's a great opportunity for Gene Simmons from Kiss to impersonate Wolfman Jack: "Wake up, sleepyheads," he whispers, before shouting, "It's party time!" Eddie though: what a lucky bastard!

Well, he was also an unlucky bastard and I also identified with Eddie on that level, because he's also a misfit who suffers at the hands of bullies at Lakeridge High School. Grammar school in England wasn't like what I see of American high school in films, but there are a number of similarities and bullies are everywhere. I was never thrown into the girls' gym naked, thank goodness, and I was never pushed, fully clothed, into a swimming pool, with a weight slipped into my backpack. How do kids ever survive American high schools? No wonder John Hughes had a movie career! I was a lot less bullied than Eddie but I still understood his pain and was firmly on his side as he sought revenge on his tormentors.

Eddie's safety net is his music, especially that of Sammi Curr, a highly successful but also highly controversial singer and guitarist who crosses off every box on the moral majority's hate list. He looks like a member of Mötley Crüe from the *Shout at the Devil* era and he writes suggestive lyrics of which they'd also be proud. He also indulges in on-stage theatrics to rival W.A.S.P., like ripping a snake apart and drinking its blood. If that has Ozzy Osbourne connotations for you, just wait until you see what *he* does in this movie! Finally, there's a Satanic edge, with backwards messages on his records, like his new album, *Songs in the Key of Death*.

Perhaps, most notably, Sammi Curr also went to Lakeridge High School a couple of decades earlier, where he was presumably also bullied. That

means that, beyond looking, sounding and acting outrageous, Sammi was a survivor. If he could make it, then so can Eddie and his personal outlet is to write to his idol, pouring out his despair and his hope for escape into words: "Sometimes, actually kind of a lot lately, I think about some pretty radical things. I've got thoughts in my head that nobody but you would understand. Why not just end it and be done with it all? Dead. Gone. But, you know something, the one that holds me together is you."

Here's where that dark edge comes in, because that reads differently today than it did in 1986. Back then, Eddie was just a troubled kid who got picked on and those were just words that set up a dumb horror movie for metalheads. Today, with a school getting shot up every ten minutes, they feel prophetic. They sound like the words of a mass shooter just waiting for a trigger moment to snap completely and take down his oppressors in a hail of bullets. Which is kind of what happens here, just with the bullets replaced by lightning bolts shooting out of the guitar of a dead metal icon resurrected through backmasking and black magic who can climb through a speaker cabinet onto a high school stage and take over the concert that's already in progress with musicians that miraculously know his material. You know, that sort of realism.

But who's dead, you might ask? Sammi Curr, that's who, in a mysterious hotel fire, and Eddie is completely devastated. He reaches out emotionally

The Awesomely Awful '80s, Part 2

to Nuke, who gifts him with the one and only acetate of *Songs in the Key of Death*. It's not out yet but Sammi wanted the Nukester to play it in entirety on WZLP at midnight on Hallowe'en as a cool debut for the album. How frickin' awesome is that?

Well, it turns out to be really awesome for Eddie because he falls asleep while playing it, dreams about Sammi Curr's death, wakes up to find that the record is skipping on a clearly backmasked section and so plays it backwards to find his idol talking to him from beyond the grave, passing on advice about how to battle his bullies. And, as he quickly discovers, that advice works. Really well. Go get 'em, Eddie!

Again, in 1986, this was awesome and hilarious all at the same time. Like Eddie writes to Sammi, "The song remains the same: total conflict, them against us." That was true, albeit without any of the sinister motives that were ascribed to us by politicians and religious leaders who didn't have a clue. The more outrageous things got, the more the normals flipped out, even more so in England than in America, where this kind of music was more mainstream. Normal people didn't understand long hair, denim and leather or studs and spikes, let alone how we could possibly be interested in horror, witchcraft or Satanism. We just thrived in not being "normal", especially when we could literally scare people by just putting on a Venom shirt and walking around in public.

The Awesomely Awful '80s, Part 2

Nowadays, it feels a little different. Nowadays, movies understand what metaphors are and they can be dramas with fantastic edges. This movie can be read metaphorically, with Sammi being an alternate personality in Eddie's tormented head, a schizophrenic voice telling him what to do and never what not to do, a little devil on his shoulder who gradually grows in power until he takes control and worse things happen to bad people. So many scenes and lines gain additional power with this reading, especially one fantastic scene where Sammi takes on Eddie's voice and they battle to respectively bring his mother into his room or keep her out. This utterly unexpected angle warrants a real reevaluation of *Trick or Treat* in light of what's going on in the current century, both in real life and on film, and it did make me wonder whether I should keep it in this book.

As those of you who follow the Awesomelys know, we started out with Awesomely Awful panels at events like Phoenix Comicon, highlighting the guilty pleasures of movies and TV, those that we know suck but still love anyway, but then we grew. Discovering the word of the eighties in *Night of the Comet*, we started Awesomely Bitchin' panels to highlight underrated gems and overlooked masterpieces. *Trick or Treat* was always awesomely awful but it's becoming awesomely bitchin' instead.

In the end, I chose to leave it in, because it's getting there through no merit of its own. The dark edge was never intended and wasn't there for

anyone to find until reality caught up. In 1986, this was awesomely awful, as perhaps personified by the scene in which Eddie tries to get revenge on his chief bully, Tim Hainey, but accidentally gets Tim's girlfriend instead.

It's a cassette, a "peace offering", that he leaves on Tim's locker the day after he saves him at the last minute from getting involuntarily trepanned by a gigantic drill in the school's metalshop. Tim throws it in his car and, after leaving a necking session on Lover's Lane to drain the lizard, Genie, his current squeeze, picks it up for a listen. It generates a weird green glow which slowly strips her naked and gets her off. Except she wakes up to find some sort of demon crouched over her, frying her brain. Off to the hospital promptly goes Genie in critical condition. In 1986, that was good clean exploitation fun.

Another aspect that's hilarious is that there are a couple of folks on the TV playing up the message that heavy metal is a sickness. One is Sylvia Cavell, president of the PTA at Lakeridge High, who successfully blocked Sammi from performing at the Hallowe'en dance on grounds of obscenity. He plucks her right through the screen of a TV, turning her into a crispy critter on the carpet of Roger Mockus, Eddie's best friend. "I'm a big fan of yours," mutters Roger. "I have all your albums." Sammi reacts in typically subtle fashion: "Shut up! Play my tape for me tonight or die!"

Mrs. Cavell is played by Alice Nunn, who's best known as Large Marge

in *Pee-wee's Big Adventure*, but Rev. Aaron Gilstrom is an even wilder choice for the casting director. "Whatever happened to the good old simple love song?" he asks. "These evil people have just got to be stopped." Who could play a character like that? Yes, it's Ozzy Osbourne himself, one of the chief inspirations for the character of Sammi Curr, which was a point of hilarity for us back in 1986. What a star! Any last words about *Trick or Treat*, Rev. Gilstrom? What's that? "This could kick you off into becoming an absolute pervert!" Fantastic.

Beyond the unintentional relevance today and the presence of Ozzy and Gene, whose images inappropriately adorn DVD covers given that they're hardly in the film, this is an awesomely awful gem that's aided by a decent script, solid effects work from Kevin Yagher and some excellent casting.

Marc Price is spot on as Eddie Weinbauer, realistic as a bullied misfit but also as the hero who's aware that it was his actions which set up the bloodshed and that he must therefore be the one to stop it. Tony Fields overplays Sammi Curr appropriately and with style that befits his history as a dancer rather than a rock musician. Doug Savant is scarily believable as Tim the bully and Lisa Orgolini is a fantastic choice for Leslie Graham, the young lady who starts to realise that what's being done to Eddie isn't funny and tries to help him, without there being an overt romantic angle. I really appreciated her part and how she played it too.

The Awesomely Awful '80s, Part 2

The one thing I haven't mentioned yet that's a huge part of this film is the music, which is a strong backdrop for the action and which was mostly provided by the band Fastway, founded by Fast Eddie Clarke and Pete Way, of Motörhead and UFO respectively. This music was good enough that the soundtrack album was worth buying on its own.

The title track has a chorus that goes like this: "Knock, knock, knockin' for a sweet surprise. It's a trick or treat." That neatly sums up the movie. It was a fun trick in 1986. Now it's a treat.

The Awesomely Awful '80s, Part 2

The Awesomely Awful '80s, Part 2

1987

The Gate
Adventures in Babysitting
Hard Ticket to Hawaii
Deathstalker II
Blind Date

The Gate

Director: Tibor Takács
Writer: Michael Nankin
Stars: Stephen Dorff, Louis Tripp, Christa Denton, Kelly Rowan, Jennifer Irwin, Deborah Grover, Scot Denton and Ingrid Veninger

Hello to 1987 and hello to another horror movie featuring a metalhead and a metal band, but this one is completely different from *Trick or Treat*. In fact, it's so different that I could actually see it in the theatre in England because it was rated 15 rather than the usual 18 and I was sixteen in 1987. I did see a lot of 18 rated films but only because I had friends who rented them and we watched them at home over a couple of beers. Back then, we could drink in pubs at sixteen but not watch horror movies until we were eighteen, horror movies that were probably also cut by the censor.

I can't remember if *The Gate* was the first horror film I saw in a theatre but it had to be close. I do remember that I loved it. It felt like a beginning to a wonderful world where I could start to see the movies I was reading about in *Fear*, *The Dark Side* and, on occasion, imported copies of *Fangoria*. However, I was definitely still a naïve sixteen year old kid. How do I know that? Because I went straight from the theatre to the record shop to order a copy of *The Dark Book* by Sacrifyx, the outrageous metal album featured in this movie as the explanation for why the gate to Hell opens up in little Glen's back yard, after a lightning strike took down his tree, and how he and his buddy Terry can close it again. Yeah, I know, I was an idiot, but it's a good way to see how invested I was in this sort of material at the time.

Glen is an annoying little kid, supposedly twelve years old and played by Stephen Dorff, earning his first credit. Every time anything happens, he wants to call mum and dad, because they've vanished for a long weekend, leaving him in the charge of his sixteen year old sister, Al. The only reason we have any sympathy for Glen is because Al is even more annoying, if for different reasons. She's the reason parents about to leave town tell their teenage kids not to hold parties the moment they leave, not just because that's exactly what she does but because she doesn't do it well. Campfire ghost stories just don't have the same impact when told around the living room table over popcorn and Pepsi. Terry was my personal hero at the time, because he doesn't merely listen to that Sacrifyx album, he acts it out, including the spoken word incantation bits, with a sheet over his head for no apparent reason. The only thing I don't get is how he manages to put up with Glen so easily.

Watching afresh in 2018, this all feels like an episode of *Stranger Things*. Is that the same font on the credits? Well, not quite, but it sure looks like it. It also feels like the same kid, the same bike and the same back yard. It's only the treehouse that's different, not that that's there for long because it comes down with the tree, leaving a huge hole underneath that exudes some cool geodes for the kids to pick up and split open. Maybe all that'll show up in season 3.

This is when weird stuff really starts to happen. It's been building for a while already: electrical issues, strange noises, flies emerging from the pit in clouds of green smoke. But now a dollar store etch a sketch magically acquires the exact sort of mysterious text in some ancient foreign tongue that nobody should ever read aloud, so guess what they promptly do? I

didn't buy into them being this stupid, especially given that Glen has just been frickin' levitated in a experiment at Al's party downstairs but then, if you remove all the stupid from horror movies, the bad guys wouldn't get a chance to do anything bad. Things get even more serious in the next scene which features Terry dancing with a vision of his dead mother, who then turns into Angus, his friend's family dog, who's now just as dead.

Fortunately, even though he doesn't have the record collection of Eddie in *Trick or Treat* and he clearly doesn't know any DJs, Terry does have the Sacrifyx album called *The Black Book*. It's a sumptuous disc, with a gatefold sleeve and a whole slew of pages in the middle. And it's while listening to it again that Terry suddenly realises that it's all about them. The hole, the blood, the levitation. All that's missing to raise the hordes of Hell is the sacrifice and Al's idiot friend with a Trans Am is going to throw Angus's body into the pit, right? Of course he is. See, if we removed all the stupid, *The Gate* would have been over almost before it began.

So no, the plot doesn't really impress but the effects do. They were the work of Randall Cook and his team. Cook has three Oscars to his name, one for each of *The Lord of the Rings* movies, but he started out in crappy horror and sci-fi flicks that did fortunately improve from *The Crater Lake Monster* and *Laserblast*. He created the dimensional animation effects in *The Thing*, was working with EEG for *Ghostbusters* and *Fright Night* and then headed

north for some Tibor Takács pictures in Canada, including this one and *I, Madman*. They're excellent effects but they're also imaginative ones. For instance, at one point the arm of a claymation demon gets cut off by a closing door, so it falls to the floor and bursts into a bunch of white worms that scurry away under the door. That's fantastic.

By the way, I absolutely adore these little minions, which were partly stop motion miniatures and partly actors in rubber suits made to look tiny through clever use of forced perspective. Whatever they are, I adore them when they're inoffensive and I adore them when they turn vicious. I adore them even more than their substantially larger cousin who inevitably shows up for the finalé and is pretty damn cool too. In fact, I'd love to not only buy a copy of that Sacrifyx album but a starter pack of the demon minions too so I could set up a breeding programme. I'd supply the whole neighbourhood. And, of course, if they're really age old hellish monsters, I wouldn't have to pay Randy Cook for a license because Satan has prior art and he won't sue because then we'd absolutely know that he exists. See, I can be a tricky bastard too. I have all the angles covered!

Takács, a Hungarian emigré to Canada, was just starting out on his film career proper here. He'd made a feature length sci-fi rock opera almost a decade prior called *Metal Messiah* and he'd directed for Canadian television including a TV movie called *984: Prisoner of the Future*, but this was his real

arrival and it allowed him to continue, through *I, Madman* and *Bad Blood* to SyFy Channel movies like *Mansquito*, *Mega Snake* and *Destruction Los Angeles*, via more surprising work like the *Sabrina the Teenage Witch* TV movie and a bundle of episodes of the show *My Babysitter's a Vampire*.

There are plenty of hints at a strong future here. Even if its both family friendly and relatively predictable, *The Gate* builds well in every direction. Glen gets a little less annoying, Terry gets even more cool—I absolutely adore the scene where he falls into the pit and has to fight off tiny demon minions of clay like he's a nerdy teen Gulliver—and even Al grows through an actual story arc to her character. Her friends, on the other hand, don't. One of them seriously says "tres uncool", rhyming "tres" with "Pez".

Another solid angle is the fact that, while the core of the story is clearly about the gate to Hell and we eventually encounter a huge frickin' demon who is endearingly nervous to be out and about in our world, that's not really what makes the film rock 'n' roll. It's not what comes out of the pit that drives the film, it's the atmosphere generated by mere proximity to it that generates a succession of often imaginative scares and shocks.

Some of them are effects driven, like the telephone that melts to avoid being used, the burning Sacrifyx album—not only can't I buy the album, I can't even buy the prop!—and the scene where the hellhole starts sucking in everything around it. Many are not, though, because they're set up as

red herrings that worked really well for me as a naïve sixteen year old but still work pretty well today, now I'm a hopefully much less naïve grandpa.

Some of them played out as just cool scenes at the time but now seem more like an attempt to mix up the subgenres and make the film a sort of horror primer for kids. Really, this is a lot of different movies in one. Sure, it's about the opening and hopefully closing of the gate to Hell, but... it's a home invasion story at heart, with almost the entire film shot inside one house. It's an exploration of the fear of responsibility, of a sixteen year old trying to prove that she's an adult when her parents aren't there to save the day. It's a coming of age movie, with a twelve year old learning that he doesn't have to call mum and dad every time anything happens because, hey, he's not a baby any more. It's a monster movie with some pretty cool monsters. It's a suspense film, built through red herrings and clever ideas. And it's a ghost story too.

Rremember that ghost story scene at Al's party early on? Sure, it felt like a stupid idea at the time, recounting some ridiculous urban legend of a dead workman being walled up in the very house that Al and Glen are living in but, as the film rolls on and the creatures of Hell start to infiltrate the household, messing with the minds of those unlucky enough to still be there, that urban legend suddenly finds life. It's been three decades since I've seen this film but I still remembered that dead workman breaking out of the walls, dragging poor Terry back in with him and then falling over and transforming into tiny minions of Satan.

Apparently, the original script was a lot more vicious. The man behind it is Michael Nankin, who had written and directed *Midnight Madness* back in 1980 and went on to do a lot of work on television. He had been recently divorced and he was unemployed and he poured all "the nastiest thoughts from my childhood" into the first draught of this script. Glen and Al were both "more mischievous"; the demons don't just plague them, they take over the town, dragging out neighbours to kill them in the streets; and the boss demon was made out of bloody entrails.

As fun as that sounds, it would have made this a different movie. What works best for me is the innocence of the whole thing, the fact that adults rarely show up and children have to save themselves using whatever they think might be right, not having the remotest experience in any of this. There are no exorcists, for instance; Terry handles that himself, reading random verses from a Bible he found. There are no construction crews filling in the hole; the kids cover it up with remnants of the treehouse. No calling in the army or the national guard or the survivalist neighbour with a convenient collection of rocket launchers; it's all down to the kids, which was really empowering for me at sixteen.

Of course, Stephen Dorff has moved on a little since this point, even if he didn't land the role of Jack in *Titanic*, a miss for which he's thankful. He even has a neck now, which certainly didn't seem to be the case in 1987. *Blade* did pretty well. And *Cecil B. DeMented*. And *Space Truckers*. And many, many other movies and TV shows.

I hope he looks back with fondness, though, at his debut role playing an annoying little kid whose tree falls down and opens up a gate to Hell. This whole thing would make a fantastic story for the grown up Glen. Can you imagine him telling it to his grandkids, albeit hopefully not in his living room with popcorn and Pepsi? I hope it's a great story too for the grown up Stephen Dorff. "When I was twelve years old, I went to this house in Canada and a whole career broke loose..."

The Awesomely Awful '80s, Part 2

Adventures in Babysitting

Director: Chris Columbus
Writer: David Simkins
Stars: Elisabeth Shue, Maia Brewton, Keith Coogan and Anthony Rapp

If *The Gate* was really about kids having to deal with whatever is thrown at them while their parents are away, then *Adventures in Babysitting* is the same movie, merely with fewer claymation demon minions and more car trouble. This is another awesomely awful favourite of mine from 1987 and a fresh viewing had me reach the same conclusion I had back then: how the heck is Maia Brewton not a megastar?

Given that you probably have no idea who she is, I should point out that she's not officially the star of this movie—that's Elisabeth Shue, known at that point for *The Karate Kid*—she's the little girl in the *Mighty Thor* helmet in the poster opposite who's hanging from Shue's neck, known at the time only for being Marty McFly's child aunt in the 1955 scenes of *Back to the Future*. The character that she plays, Sara Anderson, is the coolest frickin' kid to be found anywhere in eighties cinema—and quite possibly ever since—and I still want to give her the high five I wanted to give her in 1987 because she still deserves it.

Now, that's surely a better introduction than telling you that Shue sets the picture in motion by singing along to *Then He Kissed Me*, dancing with a teddy bear and getting dressed for her anniversary date in a room that's decorated in floral designs and a wild overabundance of the colour pink. Right? She's Chris Parker and she tells herself that, "Tonight is going to be the greatest night of your life," but, unless we're also seventeen year old girls, we're just not buying it.

We start buying it a little later once everything has started to go wrong. Firstly, Mike Todwell cancels their date because his little sister's sick and contagious and his parents are going out and he drove over alone in his

Camaro with its SO COOL license plate just to tell her in person. Now that really adds up, right? Secondly, as Chris is planning a night of depression in her pink flowery bedroom, Mrs. Anderson phones to see if she's willing to babysit their kids while she and her husband go to a business party. And thirdly, soon after the Andersons leave her in charge, her friend Brenda rings with an overblown sob story. She's downtown, at the bus station, trapped in a payphone (remember them) being hassled by the people who live in it, having run away from home with only enough money to pay the cab fare there. Oh, and her dad will kill her if he finds out.

So, just like *The Gate*, all Hell has broken loose and the kids have to take care of things while the adults are away. To make up for the lack of metal and monsters, we get a fantastic set of characters. Like Al in *The Gate*, Chris thinks she's all that but she really doesn't have much of a clue. Because the Anderson kids are gloriously manipulative creatures, they come along for the ride. That's Brad, who's fifteen and has a huge crush on Chris, and Sara, who's somewhere around ten and a comic book nut who's obsessed with the Mighty Thor. Add to the mix Brad's horndog of a friend, Daryl Coopersmith, complete with his dad's latest *Playboy* because Miss March apparently looks just like Chris, and we're in for a fun ride.

Well, that fun ride gets even more fun because everything goes wrong. Chris isn't even supposed to leave the Andersons' house in the peaceful

The Awesomely Awful '80s, Part 2

Oak Park suburbs of Chicago except maybe to take them out for Häagen-Dazs, but now they're flying down the freeway to Chi-town with eighty whole minutes for scriptwriter David Simkins to use to screw up their day with emphasis. And that's precisely what he does, carefully conjuring up all the things that your parents warn you might happen if you don't do what they tell you but somehow never does. Except in the movies.

He has a lot of fun with it too. You won't be too surprised to find that the first disaster is that they blow a front tyre on the interstate. And there isn't a spare in the boot. And it's 1987, so nobody has a cellphone. And, if we were watching carefully, we know that Chris's purse is still sitting on the Andersons' couch. No money, no license. So they wait for someone to stop and help. That turns out to be Handsome John Pruitt, a nice tow truck driver who just happens to have a hook for a hand.

This sets the stage well for the succession of disasters to follow. They're thrown into scary situations populated by scary people who turn out to be nice guys. Simkins scares them, then relaxes them and then scares them again, before bouncing them over to the next disaster. It sounds episodic and, quite frankly, it is, but quite a few characters return in clever fashion.

Perhaps the best of these is Joe Gipp. Our intrepid heroes have relaxed around Handsome John, as he's a gentleman who's going to take them to Dawson's and buy them a new tyre. Well, mostly relaxed; Daryl does ask

him about his hand and he suggests that he's keeping it safe in the glove compartment. The point is that all is well. Well, until he gets the call that there's a car parked outside his house, as he knows his wife is cheating on him, so he chases over there at high speed, throws the other man out of the window and accidentally blows out the windscreen of Chris's mum's car with his gun. Surely it's time to run! So they jump into the cheat's car, as the only other vehicle there, but it's being stolen by Joe Gipp and we're already moving into the next disaster.

Gipp, played with consummate confidence by Calvin Levels, is a young African American gentleman with a grin that won't quit. He's as cool as a cucumber and he takes the whole thing in stride, promising to drop them somewhere safe once he's taken care of some business. Why he thinks that bringing them along to the chop shop run by a lunatic mastermind known as Bleak is a bright idea, I really can't fathom, but that does neatly set up the rest of the movie.

Sequestered away upstairs while the crime lords meet to plan their bad deeds for the day, Daryl snags a fresh copy of *Playboy* to replace the one that Brad threw out of the car window, not realising that this one has more than a girl who looks like Chris on the centerfold: it also contains Bleak's notes for a Philadelphia order. "That could put us away for twenty years," says one of his henchmen. And it's now in the hands of a bunch of

kids and their babysitter, who promptly escape in spectacular fashion.

Now, they're not merely lost without either money or a vehicle—and we're reeling from the realisation that this kids' picture has a copy of *Playboy* as its McGuffin—but they're being chased by some seriously bad dudes as well. Can it get any worse? Well, of course it can, because Simkins is clearly a twisted soul who should write the next instalment in the *Saw* franchise, but I'm not going to spoil the whole movie.

I will highlight my favourite disaster, though, which happens to be the next one. Having escaped the chop shop but being chased by the criminals who run it and coming up against a dead end, they slip into the only door they can find. That just happens to be the stage door to the Silver Dollar Room, a blues club on whose stage Albert Collins is performing. "Nobody leave this place without singing the blues," he intones and he's serious. A very quiet, entirely black audience waits for the pretty little white girl to embarrass herself and, frankly, this is where the whole movie could have gone completely pear shaped. It doesn't and, even though we think it will for a moment there, it doesn't with magnificent style and we're sold on the rest of the movie before it happens, especially when the song finishes, the bad guys step up and Albert Collins leans over again. "Nobody leave this place without singing the blues."

Adventures in Babysitting, which I first saw on British television under its

occasional foreign title of *A Night on the Town*, is awesomely awful because the whole thing is completely ridiculous but we have almost as much fun as the kids do, when they look back at their nightmare of an evening and realise that it was the best night of their respective lives.

Chris Columbus must have thought it would be fun because he reviewed over one hundred scripts before deciding on this one to be his directorial debut. He was a big name at the time, but as a writer, given that he'd sold a script to Steven Spielberg, who made an obscure little film out of it by the name of *Gremlins*. Then he wrote *The Goonies* and *Young Sherlock Holmes* and was ready to direct. From here, he worked on up to *Home Alone*, *Mrs. Doubtfire* and the first two *Harry Potter* movies, as well as a host of credits as a producer that makes me seriously envy his bank balance.

I'm not sure, however, that he ever made another picture as awesomely awful as this one, though. It's over a hundred minutes long but there are no dull moments, however wildly unrealistic the action gets. And it gets amazingly unrealistic, trust me. At one point, the kids find themselves in an empty subway carriage, only for the doors at each end to open to show rival gangs ready to launch into each other over some turf war. While this is generally a polite and family friendly movie, I just can't resist quoting the rare instance of profanity that emerges as Chris and Brad find a way to escape. Well, OK, I'll quote the edited for TV version instead. "Don't fool

with the Lords of Hell," one gang boss shouts, as he hurls his flick-knife into Brad's shoe. Chris grabs it and waves it right back at that gangbanger. "Don't fool with the babysitter!" she shouts in return.

Of course, the reactions the kids give to their mild-mannered babysitter saying "fool" is hilarious because that sure ain't what she said. By the way, TV addicts, that Lord of Hell doesn't really call Chris a "witch" either. I'm sure this scene is supposed to be tense, but it's just a set-up for that classic line, which works so well when not being censored. The tense scenes are when Sara finds herself on the glass on the outside of a skyscraper, way too many frickin' levels up, trying to escape hardened criminals who have control of the rope she's hanging on. That was tense when I was a kid and it's just as tense now I'm a grandpa—in fact, maybe more so *because* I'm now a grandpa. Perspective is a powerful thing.

Perspective also leads to the most touching scene in the movie too, in which Sara meets her idol, or at least so she thinks because she's ten years old and she knows that the superheroes live in the big city. We know that the muscled blonde who descends towards them on a pneumatic lift isn't Thor but she doesn't. I had no idea who Vincent d'Onofrio was when I first saw this but he's as good here as ever, cruelly bursting her bubble until she finally gets to him and thaws his mercenary heart. It's a magic scene and I say again, how is Maia Brewton not an absolute megastar?

The Awesomely Awful '80s, Part 2

Well, it turns out that this was her last movie, of a sum total of two, but she moved back to television for a while, where she'd debuted in 1984 on an episode of *Blue Thunder*. She appeared in a few TV movies, guested on a bunch of shows and then landed regular slots on *Lime Street* and as the title character's sister in *Parker Lewis Can't Lose*. I've never seen that show but I'll certainly be seeking it out now, along with TV movies like *Sky Trackers*. She ended her career because she went to Yale and became an attorney, so I shouldn't complain that she didn't make more movies for Disney to make pointless but inevitable remakes of.

Not everything here is good, of course, because this is awesomely awful rather than just awesome. This is America; did they really think that they could go to hospital with fifty cents and no ID? The escape from the chop shop is enough to lose Chris her babysitting license for life. What the heck was she thinking? And, of course, sure as it's sunny today here in Phoenix, the script contorts itself so as to give her the opportunity to get out of her old relationship and, completely separately, into a new one. Sara's trip to the outside of a skyscraper's windows is more believable than that.

Oh, and it's not with Brad, because that would be creepy. After all, Chris is seventeen and Brad is played by an actor who's seventeen. How creepy would that be? Well, Keith Coogan, who must have liked babysitters, given that he returned four years later as Christina Applegate's stoner brother

in *Don't Tell Mom the Babysitter's Dead*, plays a believable kid. Then again, he had the perfect heritage for it; his grandfather, Jackie Coogan, played *The Kid* back in 1921 opposite Charlie Chaplin. Meanwhile, Elisabeth Shue, who we fail to buy as seventeen for a moment, was actually seven years older.

I should add a quick nod to Anthony Rapp, who gifts Daryl with just the right amount of annoyance factor and whose highly respected career in film, television and especially on stage, not least as an original lead in the musical *Rent*, deserves to be remembered without the caveat that he was the one who raised sexual harassment allegations about Kevin Spacey.

In fact, all four of the young leads are excellent and I'm shocked that, as self-contained as the film is, Hollywood didn't immediately greenlight a sequel. The closest Chris Columbus gave us to *Adventures in Babysitting II* or *More Adventures in Babysitting* are his *Home Alone* movies, which do have a few similarities here and there. Sadly, *Home Alone* starred Macauley Culkin instead of Maia Brewton. I need to find that alternate universe!

The Awesomely Awful '80s, Part 2

The Awesomely Awful '80s, Part 2

Hard Ticket to Hawaii

Director: Andy Sidaris
Writer: Andy Sidaris
Stars: Ronn Moss, Dona Speir, Hope Marie Carlton, Harold Diamond, Rodrigo Obregon and Cynthia Brimhall, Patty Duffek, Wolf Larson, Lory Green, Rustam Branaman, David DeShay, Michael Andrews, Kwan Hi Lim, Joseph Hieu and Peter Bromilow

Even though *Adventures in Babysitting* technically revolved around the search for the Miss March centerfold in a copy of *Playboy*, there were no boobs in it. The movie, that is, but maybe not even the *Playboy* prop. Hey, it was generally family friendly, even with one of the best F-bombs in the history of the movies. Boobs could easily be found elsewhere and there was never a better place to find than in an Andy Sidaris movie.

Hard Ticket to Hawaii was his fourth of twelve pictures as a director and the second of ten in his series of BBB movies (he produced a couple more that were directed by his son, Christian Drew Sidaris, who assisted here). These movies are vaguely linked but in such a tortuous way—some actors die in this series half a dozen times as half a dozen different characters—that it's only die hards who are willing to put in the effort to contort them into continuity, but they all have that common factor of BBB.

What's that, you ask? No, it's not a wild bra size, though that would be appropriate. Usually it's *Bullets, Bombs and Babes*—the title of a book on the films published by *Heavy Metal* magazine—but it can be "Bullets, Bombs and Boobs" too. The mandatory DVD box set shifts to GGG or "Girls, Guns and G-Strings". While that should be self-explanatory, I'll add that these films feature a collection of *Playboy* Playmates and *Penthouse* Pets who constituted an unusually top heavy stock company of actors.

You see, rather than casting Elisabeth Shue as someone who just looks like Miss March, Sidaris would actually cast Miss March and here he did just that with Dona Spier, as she was Miss March 1984. She's also our lead, a delivery girl of sorts but, in an Andy Sidaris movie, that means that she flies a plane for Molokai Cargo, a Hawaiian front for the Agency, for which she works as an undercover agent. Her partner is Taryn, played by Miss July 1985, Hope Marie Carlton, who's still technically a civilian but willing when it's needed. Also present are Miss October 1985 (Cynthia Brimhall) as Edy, the owner of a restaurant which the Agency uses as a central point of operations, and Miss May 1984 (Patty Duffek) as one of her waitresses, oddly named Pattycakes. That's four prominent Playmates in parts that allow them to do more than show us their parts. That's a lot of, erm, talent right there. Also gorgeous is Michele, Edy's bartender, but she's not quite what she seems, even though she is played by a bona fide beauty queen.

Now before you start thinking this is just some soft porn flick made for broadcast on Skinemax, I should point out that Sidaris has seven, count 'em, seven Emmies to his name, for his television work. He was a pioneer in sports broadcasting, directing the first quarter of a century's worth of *Wide World of Sports* on ABC. Of course, while there, he invented what he

called the "honey shot", a close-up of a cheerleader or just a pretty girl in the audience to break up the testosterone. BBB was a natural progression.

He also has a cameo in this film, though he also often floats around in the background at Edy's as if he's a real character. His conversation with a hooker who's delivered to him at his table sets the stage for the level of humour we can expect. He breathlessly pours out, "Charlotte, I'm not just some fast talking New York television director. I care for you a great deal. Trust me, Charlotte." She mentions that, "You practically raped me last night." He replies: "That was last night, Charlotte. This is today. I care for you, Charlotte. I care for your mind. I don't care for your body. I'm not into that." Enter a buxom waitress in a bikini to steal his attention and, "I'll have a pair of coffee."

What you'll be most surprised about is that the rest of the picture isn't entirely about boobs. There are plenty of those and the characters do have a knack of popping them out ten seconds after being introduced, but there is an actual story unfolding here and some of those girls are keen on living up to their action hero potential. The core of this one is about diamond

smuggling, but there's a truly bizarre subplot about a snake that I promise you will never ever forget. You could receive a hit to the head and forget your entire life but you will never forget the snake in Hard Ticket to Hawaii.

The diamonds belong to Mr. Chang, our big bad boss, who, according to the rules of American film, has to be exquisitely British. He flies them onto the island of Molokai inside a very cool remote controlled toy helicopter, controlled from his clearly expensive yacht, so that his local boys, led by Seth Romero, can grab them. Unfortunately, on this latest flight, he drops them right in front of Donna and Taryn, who don't appreciate being shot at by a couple of hoods, so they promptly hurl a pair of nunchucks and a throwing star at them. That's really impressive and I'm not talking about their aim, I'm talking about how they secreted such weapons in outfits as skimpy as the ones they're wearing!

So, most of the movie involves Chang's minions trying to recover these lost diamonds, which isn't anywhere near as straightforward as you might think, given that the bad guys know who the girls are and where they live. For one, death is never a subtle thing in an Andy Sidaris movie, so we have

The Awesomely Awful '80s, Part 2

some truly spectacular action coming. Put simply, the bad guys are batshit insane and the good guys make Rambo look like a pussy.

And then there's the snake, which I've been dying to get back to. You see, there are no snakes on Hawaii. The girls tell us that as they pick up a snake in a crate from their cover boss, Mr. Dickson, to take to the wildlife park. But, horror of horrors, there's a mix-up and they pick up the wrong snake. Yes, there are no snakes on Hawaii... except for the two different snakes which just happen to be stacked in identically marked crates in the same aisle of the same depot on the same day. To be fair, one crate did have an extra warning sign on it but that fell off when a fork lift bumped it, so what are the odds?

Amazingly, that's not the wildest point here. The snake for the wildlife park is just a routine boa constrictor, but the snake the girls pick up is a little different. Are you ready for this? Let me allow Dickson to explain: "That snake has been infected," he tells the girls, much too late for it to do any good, "by deadly toxins from cancer infested rats." He even feels the need to add, "It's a very dangerous snake." It looks it too. It's the colour of

a dozen different bruises, it hisses and spits and it looks like it's going to melt at any time. But some bright spark shipped it to Hawaii in a cheap crate which would fall to pieces if you looked at it long enough, with gaps a great deal larger than snakes need to squeeze through to escape into the gorgeous landscape of Hawaii whenever they damn well please.

But hey, this is an Andy Sidaris film so style beats up substance with nunchucks every chance it gets, which is oddly the closest these movies tend to get to substance abuse, given that they're riddled with DEA agents and narcotics smugglers. This snake is more than happy to stay in its crate until it's time for it to not stay in its crate. And eat people. When the girls discover the bodies of a honeymooning couple that they delivered to a gorgeous beachfront campsite, they're horrified and so are we because these really aren't horror movies, they're action flicks, as we're reminded when the snake finally gets his. Blowing people out of top floor windows with oversize handguns is expected. Gruesome corpses are not.

To hint at how the snake gets taken down, let me highlight another contender for the wackiest death scene in this movie. The girls have done

The Awesomely Awful '80s, Part 2

well for half the picture because Sidaris is a feminist in his way, who's very happy for his female characters to be capable ladies who kick ass and take names, just so long as they follow up by doing all their thinking topless in the jacuzzi. However, there comes a point where things get so dangerous they realise that they have to call in their boss, Rowdy Abilene, who's not that far away on his houseboat, *Malibu Express*, which had been previously owned by his brother, Cody Abilene, in the previous film, *Malibu Express*.

Rowdy and his colleague Jade, who's a male martial artist, drive to the rescue, but they're attacked on the way by a skateboarder with only two things in his arms: a machine gun and a blow up doll. I'm assuming that there's a double meaning involved here and the doll is really a bomb that will serve as a backup for this assassin in case he misses with the gun, but we don't get to that. Instead, they counterattack and I really would love to show this scene to a physics professor so I could watch his brain implode.

Clearly, this is a great maths question in the making: how fast does a star of *The Bold and the Beautiful* need to reverse his jeep in order to bounce a skateboarder and his blow up doll high enough into the air for him to

take each of them down in turn with a bazooka? A frickin' bazooka! Now you're getting pretty close to picturing the snake's death scene but you're still missing the motorbike and the wall. And the toilet. Don't even get me started on the razor frisbee of death. And don't accuse Sidaris of having a one track mind! Sure, he likes boobs, that's a given, but he also knows how to fashion death scenes that are wildly imaginative enough to make us spew our beer.

Surprisingly, Dona Speir and Hope Marie Carlton are capable leads. I've seen worse actors who were actually actors, often in big budget Hollywood movies whose female stars aren't remotely allowed to kick ass like these ones do. In fact, these female stars arguably kick ass better than their male bosses. Rowdy uses a bazooka because he can't hit anything smaller than the side of a barn with a handgun. Jade may have some decent martial arts moves but he also has a man bun that shakes embarrassingly loose every time he tries one, not that it wasn't embarrassing when it was in place but hey; if he was that dedicated to it, wardrobe should have stapled it to his scalp. The guys have much cheesier dialogue too, which is nowhere near as good as you're imagining. "Just when you thought it was safe to take a pee," is a not a line that the cinematic universe really ever needed. Maybe we can deal with "I don't want to control your life. I jut want to suck the polish right off your toes." Or maybe not.

Paste magazine ranked *Hard Ticket to Hawaii* the best B-movie of all time, which it isn't, but it is both utterly ridiculous and eminently watchable and it has a whole bunch of scenes outrageous enough to stay with you for years.

Some are so bad they're good, such as when Rowdy realises there's an armed thug just around the corner so simply blows up the entire wall with his trusty bazooka. Some, however, are so bad they're just bad, like when our collective heroes successfully complete a dangerous rescue mission on the enemy camp, only to realise that they completely forgot about the big boss, so Randy has to drive out of the back of their truck on a motorbike to go take care of him too. Here's another maths question for you: how long does it take a bad guy to break through a slatted closet door with a knife?

The Awesomely Awful '80s, Part 2

The answer, of course, is one single second longer than it takes the girl hiding inside to load her harpoon.

Perhaps most bizarrely for a picture containing a plethora of *Playboy* Playmates, the single sex scene (well, naked make out session) is definitely the most boring part. Sure, Dona Spier has a gorgeous ass, but it poses so much during this scene that it should have its own credit. I'm tempted to find me a *Playboy* Playmate to make out with, for academic reasons alone you understand, just to see how many instinctive poses she makes during. And whether the cheesy easy listening music kicks in automatically as a service provided by the universe at large.

No, this isn't the best B-movie of all time, but it's about as awesomely awful as it gets, folks. Revisiting this makes me want to play the DVD box set in entirety, pausing only if we run out of pizza and beer.

The Awesomely Awful '80s, Part 2

The Awesomely Awful '80s, Part 2

Deathstalker II

Director: Jim Wynorski
Writer: Neil Ruttenberg, based on a story by Jim Wynorski
Stars: John Terlesky, Monique Gabrielle, John La Zar and Toni Naples

One of the big surprises of *Hard Ticket to Hawaii* was that Playmates can act. No, Dona Spier isn't going to be winning an Oscar any time soon, but she's more than able to carry a feature film, looking great and kicking ass, even if a gigantic contaminated snake threatens to steal scenes from her every now and then. Jim Wynorski, making *Deathstalker II* in Argentina for exploitation legend Roger Corman, cast Monique Gabrielle, the *Penthouse* Pet for December 1982 and his then girlfriend, in not only one but a pair of prominent roles, but she sadly has the acting talent of a newborn kitten: she looks irredeemably cute as one and supremely sleek as the other but don't ask her to string more than a single line together at any one time.

Fortunately, we're not supposed to take this picture seriously at all. The other three *Deathstalker* movies are traditional sword and sorcery fantasy pictures, played straight, with other actors taking the leading role: Rick Hill and John Allan Nelson. This one however, is clearly a spoof, not only of *Deathstalker*, who's played by John Terlesky's grin—so prominently that it steals every scene from him—but also the genre as a whole, with some of the most cringeworthy lines ever committed to celluloid. It's amazing how much can be successfully trimmed away from an already skimpy budget when we're too busy laughing to notice how ridiculous the sets are.

We get one of those lines at the very beginning of the film. The opening scene has Deathstalker steal a jewel made of plastic from a stone temple made of foam, kills a garrison of guards with his swordfighting skills, even though his sword rarely touches them, and finally leaps through a latticed window to the ground, where his horse awaits, leaving his weapon behind. Enter a sorceress in a leopardskin bikini to presage the title in an odd monotone: "I'll have my revenge. And Deathstalker too." *Deathstalker II*, geddit? And right before the title card appears!

Yeah, those jokes don't get much better, but they're often so atrocious that they can't fail to make us laugh, especially when the screen is full of Terlesky's grin and Gabrielle's cuteness and especially when we're full of pizza and beer. Here's a great example. After the former rescues the latter for the second time and they hightail it out of town on his horse with guards in hot pursuit, they sneak off the path to imagined safety. "You have to get up pretty early in the morning," Deathstalker boasts to his companion, "to catch the Prince of Thieves." Then an arrow hits the tree right next to them and she points out, "It *is* pretty early in the morning!"

We're hardly into the picture and we've already run through half of the sword and sorcery cliché checklist in that one town alone. Inside just one bar are topless dancers, pig monsters and a one-eyed pirate who watches the entire place get trashed in a barfight. Well, all except the numerous barrels of beer. How do we know that they're barrels of beer, you might ask? Well, they're barrels with signs on them that read, "Beer". What did I tell you about the budget? And, of course, there are quips. Three guards ask if Deathstalker knows them. He guesses at "the village idiot and the two runners up?" He kills the first two but the third scampers away, with the line, "Hey, I don't even know those guys!" on his tongue.

The Awesomely Awful '80s, Part 2

Meanwhile, under all this cliché made bearable and often delightful by the irreverent attitude, we also have an actual story. Gabrielle plays Reena the Seer. Well, she's actually Princess Evie playing Reena the Seer, because an evil sorcerer—"Are there any other kind?" asks Deathstalker—by the name of Jarek has made an eighties glam metal copy of her soul which has usurped her throne and banished her from her own kingdom of Jafir. Now she's found Deathstalker, she uses her powers as a seer, which may well be non-existent, to talk him into keeping her safe on the inevitably long and perilous journey back to Jafir, killing Jarek and finally restoring her to the throne. It isn't too hard, she suggests, playing up how it'll get him into the legends. "Right up there with Conan."

Deathstalker—"Is that your first name or your last name?" asks Reena—falls for it, of course, and they promptly set off so that he can do all the things that swordsmen in sword and sorcery pictures tend to do: finding new friends, vanquishing new foes and getting as much action from the ladies as he can along the way, all while failing to notice that his travelling companion is the cutest little seer you've ever seen.

Oh, and falling into traps. He's surprisingly good at that, though he also seems to be pretty good at finding his way out of whatever traps he finds his way into. Now, I have to call out the equal opportunity trap setting in this movie because it's notably ahead of its time. Sure, Deathstalker is the

The Awesomely Awful '80s, Part 2

usual smug womaniser, but the various people responsible for the script—Neil Ruttenberg wrote it from a story by Jim Wynorski, but a great deal of it was conjured up when needed by the director and his leading man—were very happy for him to be captured by men or women, living or dead, whatever, just as long as they did so through suitably time honoured traps (read: clichés) that they could have fun with.

For instance, the only set seen more often in fantasy movies than the stone temple made of foam is the quarry made of rocks that can be blown up without anyone caring. Sure enough, that's the first trap here, with the one-eyed pirate assassin known as Jin attacking him there with explosive arrows a go go and a team of carefully selected characterful mercenaries.

I have to give them a shout out because they're especially wild. There's Crazy Otto Rheingold, the Mad Prussian; Ed "The Head" Shumanski (part time consultant to Attila the Hun who has also spent five years on Genghis Khan's taskforce); John "The Baptist" Mombaso ("drowning's a specialty"); Nick the Crippler of Kashmir; and Buddy "Footstool" LaRosa, a midget who "was recently dismissed by Ivan the Terrible for extreme brutality." Now, the history buffs among you may be scratching your heads because those real names aren't remotely contemporary. Attila the Hun died in 453 AD, but Genghis Khan wasn't born until 1162 and Mrs. the Terrible didn't birth young Ivan until 1530. Maybe those contributors to the script mixed up

The Awesomely Awful '80s, Part 2

Deathstalker II with *Beastmaster 2*, given that that one was subtitled *Through the Portal of Time*. I'm surprised none of these thugs had a Nazi armband.

Anyway, once Deathstalker has taken care of these morons, he falls into another trap because the laws of inevitability require it. This time, he feels that they're low on funds, so they should raid a tomb. Well, he is a thief, or at least someone in "the wealth redistribution business", as he puts it, so a mausoleum shouldn't be much of a problem. Well, Jarek is a bright one as evil sorcerers go and he's keeping tabs on the princess and her would be saviour and he's way ahead of them here, having somehow fitted the tomb they stop at with one of those crushing walls of death, this one decked out with evil looking spikes for good measure. Convenient that, huh?

Best of the lot is the tribe of Amazon women who apparently missed the memo about chopping off a boob to allow for smoother archery. Maybe they figured it would spoil the aesthetics of their bikini tops. They are aware of Deathstalker's reputation, so they immediately put him on trial. All trials here are by combat, so he's thrown into an actual wrestling ring to face the queen's champion, who appropriately goes by Gorgo, a shock for Deathstalker when he discovers that she's really Dee Booher, credited as Queen Kong and whom I remember well from *G.L.O.W.* as Matilda the Hun. It's the one sided battle you might expect, given that she's at least a foot taller than her opponent, and it's surprisingly long, but what got me

here were the ring girls.

Let's just think about this. I guess that it's fair to assume that Amazon tribeswomen in a village without a single man probably end up lesbians by default, especially in a movie aimed at a young male audience. However, these particular lesbian warriors have just found Deathstalker guilty of "crimes against womanhood". Are we really supposed to believe these proto-feminists don't find ring girls in bikinis demeaning to the not so gentler sex?

Of course, it's also weird to find ring girls in bikinis wearing some of the more sedate female outfits in the film. Toni Naples, a previous girlfriend of Jim Wynorski—clearly, director of B-movies is one of the greatest jobs in the world if you want to date beautiful women—wears a stunning little black leather number that shows off her cleavage so emphatically that it takes us a while to notice that she was clearly sponsored by a cosmetics company specialising in blush. Monique Gabrielle, in her other role as the clone princess, is generally attired in the sort of ridiculously unrealistic costumes that we all know and love from the paintings of Frank Frazetta and Boris Vallejo. The most unbelievable aspect of this entire movie is how those bras manage to stay on for the duration.

The rest of the picture is full, of course, of stunning realism. Everyone knows that resurrecting the dead has to be done under strobe light, right?

The Awesomely Awful '80s, Part 2

The best way to fire someone is clearly to run them through with a sword from the other side of a dry ice portal. Cloned princesses can't eat regular food, just the bodies of vibrant young men, and they remember them by magically incorporating them into their headboards; that's just a fantasy version of the photos of lunch on your Facebook feed, right? Naturally, the best way for the filmmakers to demonstrate to us the extent of the tunnels under the castle is to set up their camera once and let Monique Gabrielle wander back and forth through one junction for a few minutes. Oh, and, when you need to get information out of someone, the old razor sharp pendulum swinging from the ceiling never fails. That's as original as the line that accompanies it. "You don't expect me to talk?" asks Deathstalker. "No, no, no," replies Sultana. "I expect you to die." Yes, yes, yes, I confess that I've never heard that in a single James Bond movie, Sultana. It's 1274; you can sue them!

Just in case we don't quite buy into every one of these slices of dramatic genius, Deathstalker keeps on throwing quips at us like he's being played by Rodney Dangerfield—and wouldn't that be a blast? "I heard it was bad luck to walk over graves," suggests Reena as they approach the tomb they plan to rob. "I heard it was just the open ones," replies Deathstalker.

This sort of thing happens even at the most inappropriate moments. Is that a corpse chained to the side of this tunnel? Sounds like I should throw out another quip! "Looks like he died with a gag in his mouth," points out the seer. "Yeah, well if he did," adds Deathstalker, "he never got a chance to tell it." Of course, the funniest joke here is that some people apparently didn't get it and look down on this movie for its cheap sets and bad acting. They probably didn't even buy into the inevitable happy ending, bucko.

It's so self-referential that Princess Evie, once restored to her throne—come on, you didn't know that was going to happen from the beginning?—explains to Deathstalker, in her most accurate prediction as a seer, that, "A thousand years from now, players will reenact all our exploits."

According to John Terlesky on the commentary track he recorded for a DVD release, a couple of Australians also watch it every Friday night. Yes, it's that sort of movie. How awesomely awful can it get?

The Awesomely Awful '80s, Part 2

Blind Date

Director: Blake Edwards
Writer: Dale Launer
Stars: Kim Basinger, Bruce Willis, John Larroquette and William Daniels

There are two very different kinds of screen comedy: the sort where we're supposed to laugh with the characters we're watching and the sort where we're supposed to laugh at them. *Blind Date* starts out as the former but pretty quickly turns into the latter and there's a real sadism at points built out of the attitude that I no longer care what happens to me as long as I can make your life a living hell in the process. I think that puts *Blind Date* notably ahead of its time with its humour.

Initially, we're entirely on the side of our unlucky protagonist, Walter Gates, in the form of Bruce Willis, way back when he still had hair, hadn't yet thrown anyone off the Nakatomi Tower and was still believable as an everyman. Much of the reason is that he's someone who gets things done, as against someone who really can't be bothered to do anything but gets away with it every time because he's smoooooth. I know I've found myself on the wrong side of that comparison and I'm sure you have too. Here, it applies to Walter and Denny, colleagues at a company with neither a name nor a soul. We have no idea what they do, but it has something to do with money and accounts and schmoozing, so they're emphatically on the dark side of American business, presumably stealing from the many and giving to the few.

They meet before an important morning meeting. Walter was at work until three in the morning, he didn't get much sleep—he looks like death warmed up—and he's struggling to get all his data together in time to present it. Denny, on the other hand, was getting it on with a lady in a limo last night, while he was standing up with his head out of the sunroof, crowing at the stars. He even has pictures. He hasn't done any preparation

The Awesomely Awful '80s, Part 2

whatsoever and can't answer any questions about his part in things but he looks really sharp in his expensive suit and so Walter's the bad guy.

"Image is everything," explains Harry Gruen, their boss, and that's very important right now because an Japanese industrialist called Yamamoto is about to entrust all his accounts to their company, so they need to make a good impression at an upcoming dinner in his honour. He has really old fashioned morals, so old fashioned that he has a silent wife in traditional geisha garb who does his every bidding while he maintains concubines all over the place. That's why Harry is worried about Walter and his date. He isn't bringing the embalmer again, is he?

Ah yes, we've got to the point of the movie. Walter needs a date for the dinner tonight and Susie Davis, his brother's wife and his usual go to fake date, is unavailable, so he has to accept a blind date instead with one of her cousins, who's back in town, living out of a hotel and looking for new friends. Given that Nadia Gates is played by Kim Basinger, in her prime one year after *9½ Weeks* and two before *Batman*, we might be forgiven for assuming that he's going to have a wonderful time. Wouldn't you? Well, if he did, we wouldn't have a movie. Nadia is perfect, explain Ted and Susie, except for one little thing...

No, she doesn't have two heads and she doesn't swear like a sailor and she doesn't have a laugh like a cackling hyena. She just goes a little crazy when she drinks. "Don't get her drunk," Susie emphasises over the phone. "She loses control completely." The problem is that she's warning Walter through Ted, who has a wry grin on his face as he passes on his version of

her words. She loses control, wink wink, nudge nudge, know what I mean! Sure enough, before they've even got to the dinner, Walter, who's such an inveterate workaholic that he probably hasn't seen a woman except for his secretary in a couple of years, has stopped for a bottle of champagne and cajoled her into one little glass. "I don't think I should drink," Nadia reinforces. That's before she takes it, of course. After it, she's all over him like she's had one little bottle instead. She's not just a blind date, she's a blind drunk date.

To suggest that dinner is one great big disaster is an understatement for the ages and the sheer joy for us is trying to figure out how all the little disasters can keep on compounding to create the biggest big disaster that they possibly can. This is director Blake Edwards on very familiar ground because he did this sort of thing for years in the *Pink Panther* movies and a whole bunch of others.

It starts mildly, of course. She pulls flowers out of an expensive display after entering the posh French restaurant. She slips in her high heels and accidentally rips Walter's pocket right off his suit jacket. Her Baton Rouge accent comes to the fore, along with a notable lack of inhibitions. She tells some bad jokes. Nothing too serious, right?

Well, trust me, it escalates. When Denny wanders over and asks about Walter's pocket, she rips his off too. When he slips her his card, she loudly calls him on it, then goes and tells his date. She insults the snobby French waiter in his own language and happily translates his responses. When he moves, she accidentally drenches Walter's boss with champagne. Then she

goes over to chat with Mrs. Yamamoto. It isn't Nadia who knocks her wig off, though that happens, but it's absolutely Nadia who follows her into the bathroom and suggests to her that, under California law, she's entitled to half her husband's assets. Returning to the dinner party, she announces that Yamamoto is worth $100m and his wife needs a good divorce lawyer. A great finishing touch is that half the gentlemen there stand up.

This all unfolds in a few short minutes and, needless to say, Walter is promptly fired. "I only wish I was in the army," Harry Gruen tells him, "so I could have you shot. Twice." Some movies would have ended here, with Walter feeling like his life already has, but this is just the beginning, not only to our story but to a rather memorable night.

Oddly, neither Bruce Willis nor Kim Basinger are much of the reason why it's memorable. While she's the lead and he was earning his first big screen credit alongside her, I'd suggest that *Blind Date* is more of a John Larroquette movie. Like Willis, he was known at this point primarily for television rather than film. Willis, two movies away from stardom in *Die Hard*, was, along with Cybill Shepherd, already a huge TV star because of the show *Moonlighting*. Larroquette had made a dozen films, from *Stripes* to *Twilight Zone: The Movie*, and he had provided the narration for his friend Tobe Hooper's *The Texas Chain Saw Massacre*, but he was still best known for the show *Night Court*. He had even asked the Emmy committee that he be no longer considered for any future awards, after winning a record four Primetime Emmys in a row. Eventually, he'd win again, for *The Practice*. That isn't surprising because he's absolutely fantastic here.

The Awesomely Awful '80s, Part 2

Perhaps, when Kim Basinger destroys her date's life and career in one swell foop at dinner, we might be forgiven for thinking that Larroquette had already come and gone. With some time to kill before dinner, Walter had taken Nadia to a couple of other places, to break the ice as it were. Pressuring a glass of champagne on her was during their second stop, at a music studio he knows where the fascinating jazz guitarist Stanley Jordan was tapping his fretboard. Before that was an art gallery recommended by Susie. It's a weird place, very Giger-esque, but they don't just find bizarre art there, they also find Nadia's "psychotic ex-boyfriend, Dave", who takes less than a minute to live up to that billing, throw a bad punch and get his arm stuck in an exhibit.

Fortunately for the movie, that's not the end of David Bedford, because it would be a lot less fun if he wasn't so prominent. It's fun, for instance, when Nadia tries to get it on with Walter while he's driving. At 55mph. On the freeway. But it's a lot more fun when he pulls over and Dave pulls over right behind him to pick up his stream of consciousness string of abuse from where he left it back at the gallery. Walter cleverly gets into Dave's car, sets it in motion then jumps out and lets the batshit crazy loon chase after it. He catches up with it just in time to crash into an exotic pet store. Continuing on from there, a monkey covers his eyes at the perfect wrong moment and he crashes into a paint store. He's a real character. He could just as viably make four for bridge or three in a pitched battle between Inspector Clouseau and his manservant, Kato.

I won't spoil what else he'll be in this film, because he has a lot of time

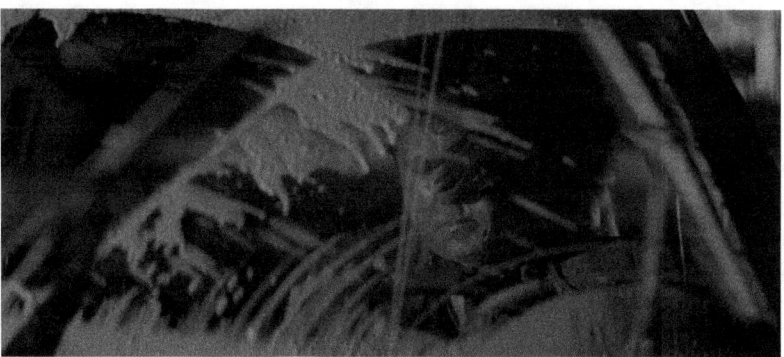

left to build and the revelations still to come are hilarious. Suffice it to say that he becomes a lot more involved after the balance of power shifts and Nadia sobers up. Again, we might be forgiven for thinking that this is the point where the movie ends, as Walter can drop her back at her hotel, hunt down and kill his brother, disown his in-laws and curl up inside a bottle for the rest of his life. However, that's not what he does. Instead, he turns the tables on her with magnificent effect.

And here's where it gets a little sadistic, especially to 21st century eyes looking back at the dark ages of 1987. After all, Walter was told not to let Nadia drink and Nadia herself told him that she shouldn't do it either. But he did the man thing, as wussy as he seems to be, and he paid the price for it. In another picture, we might be sympathetic to the poor sap but not in this one. I was sympathetic to Nadia instead. The poor girl has some sort of chemical imbalance that means that she's allergic to alcohol or some similar disorder. Yes, that's a real thing, as horrifying as it is to consider. So when we do a switcheroo and Walter takes it upon himself to ruin her life just like she ruined his, we find that we're not on his side any more.

The only reason we might find our way back onto his side is because the other side becomes psychotic ex-boyfriend Dave, who would be endearing in his insanity if only he didn't do some of the things that he'll soon do in this movie. After all, John Larroquette displays all the charisma that Bruce Willis couldn't as Walter. There is an interesting character inside Walter but he's too obsessed with other things to let him come out. And, even as a victim, Kim Basinger can't really sell Nadia to us. She's either as drunk as a

skunk and causing chaos or she's sober and miserable because she was just as drunk as a skunk and causing chaos. Those are her two faces: wild party animal and sad possum. There's nothing in between.

And, of course, if you weren't paying attention during the eighties, this isn't just a situation comedy, it's also a romance. Part of the fun, when we aren't watching John Larroquette drive into something new, is attempting to figure out just what the heck Blake Edwards and his team of writers will have to do to contort their script far enough to allow these two characters to be together by the end of the picture. They succeed, of course, but I'm sure I'm not alone in not buying it. Hey, count the hours they've spent together, subtract the hours in which one was doing a great job at pissing in the other one's cornflakes and you have not a heck of a lot at all.

It's easy to see what's wrong with this movie but, like Roger Ebert wrote at the time, when it's funny it's really funny. Most of the films I've covered in this book are awesomely awful because they're stupid but fun. This one isn't stupid so much as it couldn't figure out how to take the IQ test, but it still contains a great deal of fun, especially if you're a sadistic puppy who likes seeing people get what they deserve.

"Hi, I'm Hal and I'm a sadistic puppy who likes seeing people get what they deserve."

"Hi, Hal!"

1988

Bloodsport
Hell Comes to Frogtown
Dead Heat
Hollywood Chainsaw Hookers
Action Jackson

The Awesomely Awful '80s, Part 2

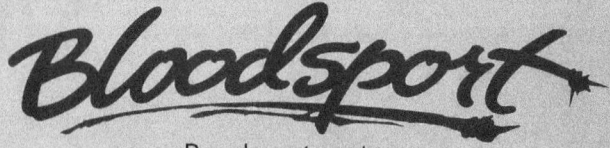

The Awesomely Awful '80s, Part 2

Bloodsport

Director: Newt Arnold
Writers: Sheldon Lettich, Christopher Cosby and Mel Friedman, based on a story by Sheldon Lettich
Stars: Jean-Claude van Damme, Donald Gibb, Leah Ayres, Norman Burton, Forest Whitaker and Bolo Yeung

If the worst film I've covered in this book is *Gymkata*, a movie about a made up martial art, then the best may be this one, a movie about a made up martial artist. It's not that it's good, but it is at least iconically bad. The action, the dialogue, the characters, even the very concept, are all exactly right if you happen to be a twelve year old boy who gets beaten up every day at school. From that standpoint, it simply couldn't be better.

The lead character is Frank Dux, a U.S. marine trained by a Japanese ninjutsu expert, who defies orders to go to Hong Kong and compete in an underground full-contact tournament of martial arts called the Kumite, for the honour of his *shidoshi* or master. This three day event, which takes place on Chinese soil but is reached through the back alleys of Hong Kong, was originated by the Black Dragon Society as a testing ground for their fighters, and is now held every five years as an invitational event to which the best and most notable martial artists in the world, of any discipline, are invited. There are no rules, fights can be to the death and the winner receives both great honour and a neat katana. It's quintessentially cool.

So far, so good. Well, Frank Dux is based on a real person called Frank Dux, who runs (or at least ran at the time) a couple of ninjutsu schools in Los Angeles. To be fair, his martial arts skills are apparently notable, but that's far from all that he advertises. As his brochures explain in detail, he's a hero, "one of the most decorated veterans of the Southeast Asian conflict", who achieved amazing feats during his time in service.

How amazing, I hear you ask? Well, he crawled through a minefield to rescue an Asian baby that he later handed over to a Taoist priest. Another time, when all was lost, he charged an enemy gun installation on his own and killed over a hundred men by himself, singlehandedly turning defeat into victory. He even rescued a boatload of orphans from Filipino pirates. What a guy!

Oh yeah, and he fought in and won the Kumite when it was held in the Bahamas, retiring undefeated after 329 matches in six years. He still holds four world records, including the most consecutive knockouts, numbering 56. This film ends with a quick rundown of all of these records, just so we can recognise what a superhero the man is.

Well, needless to say, he made all of this up and there's a truly hilarious article that was published in the *Los Angeles Times* a month after *Bloodsport* was released that debunks every one of his selling points with style. For intance, staff writer John Johnson checked his military record and found that the furthest the real Dux got to Southeast Asia was a base in San Diego and his only known war injury was when he fell off a truck he was painting in the motor pool. Check it out and laugh your ass off.

What gets me is how anyone needed that article to realise that this was fictional. Sure, we couldn't just bring up Snopes on our smartphones back in 1988, but c'mon! I was a naïve seventeen year old kid when I watched this on original theatrical release in England and I didn't buy into it then.

The Awesomely Awful '80s, Part 2

It seems utterly ridiculous now that I'm an aging grandfather.

After all, the Kumite is supposedly co-sponsored by the IFAA. Hang on, what? An international body is sponsoring an illegal underground death match in mainland China, at which the only non-Asians are either fighting in the tournament or looking incredibly obvious in the audience? Which IFAA? The Indiana Field Archery Association? How about the International Folk Art Market? Perhaps it's the International Federation of Associations of Anatomists? They would surely know where the most vulnerable points of the human body are, right? If we buy into this, maybe we'd buy into the World Boxing Association quietly running bare knuckle bouts with gypsy fighters in the basement of some abandoned warehouse in the Bronx. Or maybe that's just another frickin' movie. As it turns out, the real IFAA is based in Frank Dux's house. Because, you know, it would be.

Oh, and the Kumite is a secret tournament. Nobody's supposed to know about it, except everyone does. And they only invite the very best fighters in the world, but they don't recognise them when they show up, so they have them prove their worth right then and there, just to be sure they aren't going to die in the ring. Except they do, of course, in numbers that are surprisingly small given the amount of mismatches in the first round.

And how do they know about these world fighters anyway? There's one African fighter who runs around the jungle in a loincloth, leaping onto

trees and breaking open coconuts with violent hand chops. How do they know about this dude? He doesn't even have clothes; I'm not buying into him responding to their e-mails. And what about Ray Jackson, the other American fighter, a big burly biker who wouldn't recognise a martial arts move if it bit him on the nose? He's a big guy who can certainly brawl but in what reality does that get him an invite to a tournament of the greatest martial arts fighters in the world, let alone into the quarter finals?

If you can somehow get past all this, how about the utterly non-existent security for an illicit triad-run underground killfest? There's a journalist, inevitably blonde and beautiful, who wants to write a story on the Kumite, but, after Dux won't take her there, even after she sleeps with him for her story, she eventually finds her way in on the arm of some Asian gambler. By day three, she just saunters in on her own, just like the two military cops who were tasked by Dux's C.O. to bring him home. How did they get front row seats for the semi-finals? Nobody checked tickets? They can't claim all westerners look alike; these two aren't even the same colour.

So yeah, I have no idea how anyone bought into this being real, but it's outrageous fun from beginning to end. It was outrageous fun when I first saw it on the big screen in Halifax, when the 35mm film snapped partway through the final bout between ultraheroic Frank Dux and ultravillainous Chong Li. It's still outrageous fun today, after uncountable viewings, and I've often wondered about why that is.

The Awesomely Awful '80s, Part 2

I think one part of it is that it's the archetypal fairy tale of manhood: a dorky kid with a terrible accent achieving against great odds: to be trained by a Japanese ninjutsu master, even after the death of his son; to serve his country in the U.S. marines; to fight in battle with honour against the best of the best and win out against them all. It's the dream of every twelve year old bullied misfit who wants to fight back but somehow remain the good guy even as he does it. But there are other films that do that. What this one does is to craft every character out of an archetype.

Dux is so one dimensional that he could be in a Disney movie, if they ever decided to allow their princesses to do the splits and punch the other guy in the nuts with the death touch. He's so good that he saves the girl from a misogynistic Arab who wants her to come to his room. He's so good that he can run away from the military cops chasing him through the streets of Hong Kong and have a damn good time playing with them. He's so good that he even beats the big brawling biker in his very first game of *Karate Champ* (though maybe that's because it's set to single player).

And how about that brawling biker? His name is Ray Jackson and, the first time we see him, he's climbing onto the Hong Kong tram that Frank is riding, in his Harley Davidson shirt and backward baseball cap, drinking a can of cheap beer. He sits behind a Chinese lady, puts his feet up over the back of her seat and asks, "Baby, want to go out with a real big man?" He's

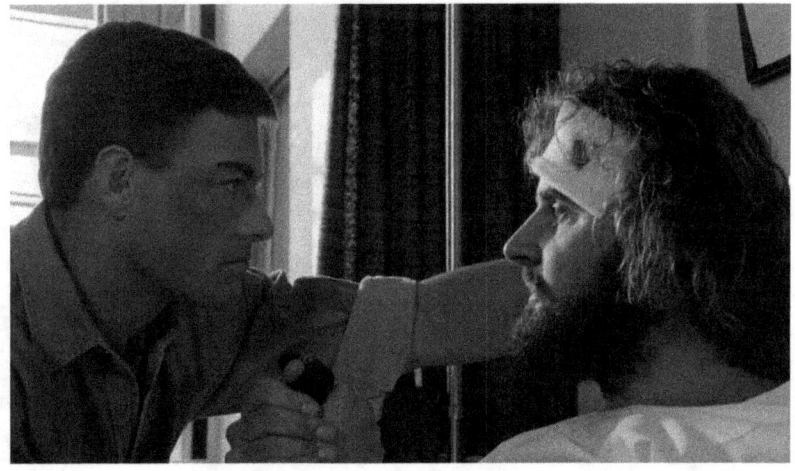

the quintessential obnoxious American, but he has a heart of gold and when he pledges to Dux that, "Anytime, any place, anywhere, if you ever need me, I'll *be* there," we feel it, man. Sure, he's an idiot and the whole three day relationship is undeniably homoerotic, but we still feel it. He's the undying sidekick, the Robin to Dux's Batman, and he'll always be.

The most archetypical character of all, however, has to be Chong Li, the villain of the piece. He's the current champion, he holds all the records and he killed a guy during the last Kumite. Jackson reiterates this: "Yeah, he kicked the poor bastard right in the throat. Chong Li stood there and watched him die." And, because Chong Li is played by Bolo Yeung, he's a prowling mass of muscles who flexes his pecs and stalks his prey with an evil sneer because nobody has ever done that better than Bolo.

Amazingly, he was 42 when *Bloodsport* was released. It had been fifteen years since he played Bolo in *Enter the Dragon*, the character from which he took his stage name; three more since he started a prolific film career, as a string of heavies and bad guys; and perhaps three more again (depending on which report you choose to trust) since he first won the Mr. Hong Kong bodybuilding tournament, a title he apparently held for ten years.

This may be his most iconic performance, not just because it's overtly villainous and he plays into it with fervour, but because every movement is calculated. There's a fantastic conservation of energy in how he moves.

The Awesomely Awful '80s, Part 2

It's there in his fighting, of course, but also, at a number of points, in the way he sits waiting, watching everything and reacting to challenges and threats with subtle motions of his head or eyes. When he defeats Jackson, he steals his bandana to wave at Frank. "You broke my record," he taunts. "Now I break you. Like I broke your friend." And so off to the hospital goes Jackson, while off to the bad guy hall of fame goes Chong Li.

And, inevitably, when he finally meets his match, which, naturally, is Frank Dux in the final, he's not man enough to take defeat graciously; he becomes the bully who has to cheat to win, crunching a pill into powder and throwing it into Dux's eyes, blinding him, a utterly obvious act that apparently nobody watching the fight is aware enough to notice. If Dux is a kick ass Disney princess, then Chong Li has to be a bodybuilding Cruella de Vil, a Maleficent with flexing pecs, or best of all, a whispering Scar, burning to stay king and willing to literally kill his opponents to retain that throne.

I should emphasise here that every one of these archetypes is a man, because women don't matter in this world. Within the large and sprawling cast, there are perhaps only two women who speak: Lily Leung in a very brief role as Mrs. Tanaka, the wife of Frank's shidoshi; and Leah Ayres as Janice Kent, the journalist, who's so fundamentally crucial to this script's progression that it can't be bothered to even give her a name for most of

the movie. What sort of homoerotic display of machismo needs women?

Janice is the only character here who isn't an archetype, but that's only because she's worthless. One minute, she's the dedicated journalist eager to tell the story of the Kumite, the next she's a flouncing wuss trying to convince the Hong Kong police (whom she fails to realise would be out of their frickin' jurisdiction) that it's violent and so should be shut down, only to then get back on board again, sitting in the front row all a flutter while her boy Frank fights in the final. Chong Li is the villain but at least he's honest about his villainy; Janice is just a pain in the ass story whore who's unaware how annoying she is and how little purpose she actually has. "Why will nobody talk about the Kumite?" she pouts. Erm, because, as you've ably just pointed out, it's a "secret full-contact event". Does this journalist really not understand the meaning of the word "secret"?

Fortunately, she's the only annoying aspect to the film because even the stupidity is endearing and that's a good thing because there's a heck of a lot of it, all of it brought to life in suitably iconic fashion. For instance, there's the dim mak scene. Dux is representing Senzo Tanaka, his shidoshi, but he doesn't look remotely Japanese so they have him show them the dim mak. That's the eastern name for the "death touch" (or, as I heard it, the even more appliable "deft touch"), where Dux has to crush the brick at the bottom of a stack of five without damaging any of the others. It's

utterly ridiculous, of course, but it makes for great cinema. It also gives Chong Li the opportunity to say, "Very good. But brick not hit back," in a direct homage to *Enter the Dragon*.

In most films, the military cops, who fly to Hong Kong to take our kick ass hero back home before he hurts himself, would be acutely annoying. Here, they're not because the casting director did well enough to hire Forest Whitaker and Norman Burton. The former is gloriously impatient and rude, without ever quite becoming obnoxious, and the latter is even better as a voice of reason who continually overrides his junior partner with respect and politeness. They're a fantastic double act, who somehow manage to be capable in everything they do as long as it doesn't involve Frank Dux, around whom they're utterly inept instead.

Finally, of course, there's the splits. Nobody expects a Jean-Claude van Damme movie nowadays without at least one instance of him doing the splits. This one has seven, I believe, including some notable examples. One comes early during the predictable but still quintessential training routine in which Shidoshi Tanaka ties Frank to a couple of trees, both wrists and ankles, and waits for him to conjure up the inner power to rise up and pull the whole thing down. Another has Jackson walk into Frank's hotel room and find him centering himself while doing the splits on a pair of chairs. "That hurts me just looking at it," he comments. "You might wanna have kids one of these days."

And if you have kids one of these days, remember to play this movie for them, around the age of twelve. It could change their life.

The Awesomely Awful '80s, Part 2

Hell Comes to Frogtown

Directors: R. J. Kizer and Donald G. Jackson
Writers: Randall Frakes, based on the story by Donald G. Jackson and Randall Frakes
Stars: Roddy Piper, Sandahl Bergman, William Smith, Rory Calhoun, Nicholas Worth, Kristi Somers, Edye Byre, Cliff Bemis, Danelle Hand and Cec Verrell

Sci-fi movies got pretty weird in the eighties and one of the key people responsible for that was Donald G. Jackson. While many filmmakers wrote futures in post-apocalyptic landscapes, it was only Jackson who populated them with rollerblading ninjas, Kabuki mimes and/or mutant amphibians.

This is the man who made a comedy feature called *Rollergator*, all about a jive-talking purple alligator who faces off against Charlie Sheen's uncle, Joe Estevez. You know, that old chestnut. Most of the time Jackson didn't even use scripts, because he and his regular partner in crime, Scott Shaw, specialised in zen filmmaking, which meant they made things up as they went along and draped them in so called artistry. He's a real trip.

Hell Comes to Frogtown, whose very name has entered pop culture deeply enough to be referenced by all sorts of people who have never seen it, has to be his best picture, partly because Scott Shaw hadn't showed up yet and partly because it was written by Randall Frakes, who wrote, produced and directed *Xenogenesis* with James Cameron. He also penned *The Terminator* and *Terminator 2: Judgment Day*, but only the novelizations, not the movies. The movies he got to write were usually for Don Jackson, like this one and *Roller Blade Warriors: Taken by Force*.

You have to like his ideas though. He begins *Hell Comes to Frogtown* with the destruction of our entire race through nuclear war. "In just ten days," the narrator tells us, "ten thousand years of human progress was virtually blown to dust. Ten years later, they tried again." After that upbeat start,

The Awesomely Awful '80s, Part 2

he demonstrates just how much fun he plans to have with this setting by recreating the Statue of Liberty scene from the end of *Planet of the Apes*, merely with a gift shop-sized model that's being scavenged by a greener, one of a new race of humanoid frogs that evolved in the radioactive wake of the war and are now restricted to mutant reservations. I'm not sure if that's social commentary or blatant racism, but I doubt it's either. I think it's just one of Jackson's many fetishes.

Then he introduces our star, wrestler "Rowdy" Roddy Piper, the same year he made *They Live* for John Carpenter. He doesn't get time to chew bubblegum here; he's pretty set straight to kicking ass. As we meet him, he's tied up and being beaten by Captain Devlin, who's rather upset about what his captive did to his daughter, only to find the man promptly freed and enlisted because he got her pregnant.

You see, in this wasteland of a future, the male population has been reduced by two thirds and most of the human race is now sterile. If Sam Hellman, who inevitably goes by Sam Hell for most of the movie, can get a woman pregnant, he can contribute to the war effort by impregnating all the other fertile women the provisional government can rustle up. You see, the war is still on, merely on pause. Each side is trying to recover its population first so they can send it at the enemy and prove that, I don't know, the third time's the charm or some such.

Unfortunately, for all this talk of fertile women, there aren't too many

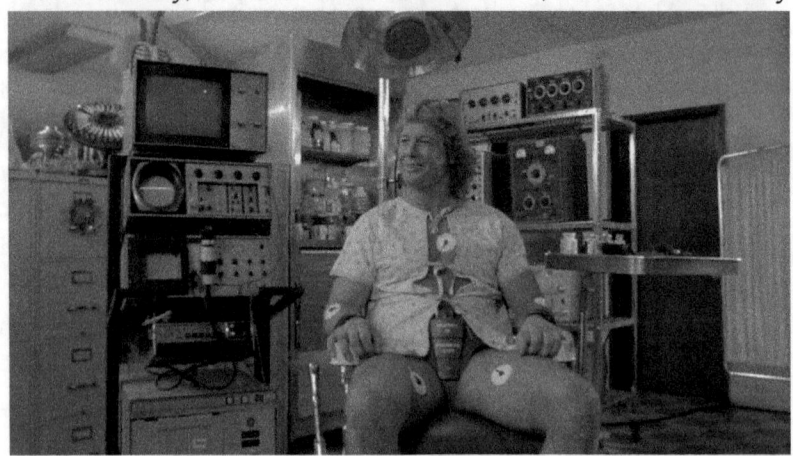

The Awesomely Awful '80s, Part 2

of them left and the last bunch they had have been stolen away and taken to Frogtown, way out in one of those mutant reservations. So off goes the newly enlisted Sam, with his spermatozoic count now a military asset, in a pink MedTech van. He's under the command of Spangle, his cute but dorky tech in glasses, with Corporal Centinella, a tough as nails guard and gunner, pledged to protect them. Spangle explains the mission to Sam in memorable terms. "We're gonna get 'em out and then you're gonna get 'em pregnant."

Now, I should add a couple of things here.

One is that Spangle, whatever rank she happens to be, is played by Sandahl Bergman, who had made a name for herself earlier in the decade as the sidekick in *Conan the Barbarian*, the title character in *She* and the villain in *Red Sonja*. She has a lot of fun here, not least when she's forced to dance the Dance of the Three Snakes for the beast in charge of Frogtown, Commander Toty. Why three snakes, you ask? Well, he has three snakes between his legs and they really like it when the dance is danced well! Oh, but she's clothed, albeit revealingly, because she had a no nudity contract.

The other is that, at this point at least, she's in total charge and she knows it. It's not just that she's really tall—she always describes herself as being 5' 12", because "no girl should have to be six feet tall"—but because Sam has been fitted with an ECR, a sort of hi-tech chastity belt. It doesn't stop him doing his military duty (or relieving himself as needed), because

it does have a flap, but it stops him from running away because it also has a proximity sensor; if he gets too far away from Spangle, its electronic stinger kicks in and no man wants to feel that amount of pain in his meat and two veg. Oh, and if he tries to remove it, there's an ounce of plastic explosive embedded within it that might just change his mind.

Now, as you can imagine, Sam jumped at the chance to be put to work impregnating every fertile woman they can find. Wouldn't you? Well, he didn't read the small print, hence the ECR, and, when he literally throws his contract out of the window of their pink truck, the girls dump him out and drive away; he's forced to run to keep up and so avoid a rather more unwanted explosion in his pants. The women are in charge! #feminism.

All this and we haven't even got to Frogtown yet. In fact, we have a set of bizarre sex scenes to get through before we get that far. Firstly, Spangle seduces him only to trigger that electronic stinger; it's all orders, she says, to keep his virility up. Then, Centinella jumps in the sack with him, as he's become a legend in his own lunchtime, only to be dressed down for being, well, dressed down. Finally, they find one of these fertile women running through the desert, the sole escapee from Commander Toty's regime at Frogtown. Spangle injects her with a drug to aid procreation and expects Sam to go to work, just like that. "You can start now," she tells him.

Can you think of another movie where the studly hero gets to suggest to his leading lady, "Maybe you ought to try making love to a complete

stranger in a hostile mutant territory. See how you like it!"? Me neither.

Eventually, of course, we do get to Frogtown and it's actually quite fun because the creature effects are pretty fantastic. No, don't take that as an implicit recommendation of *Rollergator*. Sexy dancing frog women in the Frogtown bar are in a whole different league to the rappin' purple gator being chased by a skateboarding ninja. Don't even go there. Trust me.

Much of what goes on from here could be described in similar terms to any other post-apocalyptic movie from the eighties in which the bad guys make their base in an abandoned industrial complex. It's all dressed up in wastelander style with an abundance of netting and dry ice, everyone hangs out at the toxic bar and the most fun anyone has is when bartering. If you meet a wastelander and he doesn't say that his principal hobby is bartering, he's simply not hardcore enough. The frog who's in charge of bartering here, by the way, is Leroy, who wears a frickin' fez. How cool is that? A humanoid frog in a fez! He's so quintessentially cool that he even gives Sam a real beer. Only mildly radioactive.

There's also the inevitable friend from the past—Rory Calhoun playing Lonnie O'Toole, better known as Looney Tunes—and the just as inevitable fifth columnist working to help them from inside, here a horny dancer by the name of Arabella. Oh, and she's a frog, in case you perked up just then, with three hours of make-up a day to put on her face and another half hour a day to remove it. She rescues Sam at one point and knows exactly

The Awesomely Awful '80s, Part 2

how he could thank her; he finds a sack to put over her head first, the ungrateful bastard.

And, of course, there's the man in charge—or the frog in charge, as it turns out. He's Commander Toty and he's a badass amphibian with a neat little harem of fertile women to make him happy. Why, I have no idea, as he's of a completely different species, but hey, those are the rules, I guess. I thought Princess Leia looked great in her slave outfit, personally, but I still don't get how Jabba the Hutt would. Don't think too hard on that, by the way; it gets really creepy really fast and I honestly don't want to steal away any magic from your childhood. Go watch *Howard the Duck* again.

I'm sure that, from that set-up, you can figure out how the rest of the script is going to progress, at least within Frogtown, and you'd be pretty close. However, this time out, it's done with a neat sense of humour. The codeword, for instance, that allows Spangle to recognise the inside girl is, "I love you," which, when spoken by a humanoid frog who looks like Zsa Zsa Gabor had plastic surgery to turn into Carmen Miranda, is stunningly frightening to both the characters and to us.

Also, we know that Sam shouldn't take off his ECR, but what if one of Commander Toty's henchmen—it may have been Bull, the tough one who populated his harem, but hey, they all look alike to me—decides to remove that device with a chainsaw? I was always a big fan of Hotrod in the ring but it's surprisingly cathartic to watch him squirm in his chains while the

sparks fly around him. I think it's because he's so expressive with his face and so good with the virtual panic button. His best acting has always been when his characters are in deep trouble.

There is a subplot buried in here, by the way, but it's so inconsequential that I'm not even going to explain to you what it is. It's hardly even set up, so the eventual reveal results in a collective shrug from the audience. It's merely something that happens after they escape from Frogtown, because of course they do. How could they get to all the other mandatory sections of post-apocalyptic cinema in the eighties if they didn't. How could there be a wastelander vehicle chasing them through the desert, for instance, with requisite big wheels and rocket launcher if they don't escape?

And we have characters to develop. The inevitable sad loss has to come after an escape. The just as inevitable boss battle could have happened in Frogtown, but there are no cliffs there so the filmmakers had to make that slight adjustment to our expectations. And, of course, the inevitable happy ending needs some space to choreograph, so yeah, they escape. Originality isn't this one's strong point, though I do find it odd saying that when there was a humanoid frog in a fez trying to buy Sandahl Bergman for fifty lilies.

Lets just say that the story is far from original, but the characters that populate it are as wildly imaginative as anything Don Jackson conjured up elsewhere, even if he didn't choose to include any skateboarding ninjas in this particular post-apocalyptic future. There's plenty of room in his other three dozen movies for them, at least when he's not focusing on lost sea serpents, mischief-making ghosts or mime assassins. Yes, he directed one movie called *Mimes: Silent But Deadly*, in which Mime-Girl plays herself as a deadly assassin. Because, you know, why not?

Welcome to the wonderful world of Donald G. Jackson, folks. If you're a fearless explorer into the awesomely awful, he's a great filmmaker to find. Just stick to *Hell Comes to Frogtown* and *Roller Blade Warriors: Taken by Force*, because the rest of his films will surely fry your brain. Oh, and don't pay too much for them. "High bid five, flatlips."

The Awesomely Awful '80s, Part 2

Dead Heat

Director: Mark Goldblatt
Writer: Terry Black
Stars: Treat Williams, Joe Piscopo, Lindsay Frost, Darren McGavin, Clare Kirkconnell and Vincent Price

I have no idea how I missed out on *Dead Heat*. It's a New World picture that mixes the buddy cop genre with the horror movie, wraps them into a comedy, and populates it with supporting actors like Keye Luke, Darren McGavin and Vincent Price. It's the sort of feature that I'd have grabbed off the rental shelves in a heartbeat in the early nineties. However, it took Britt Rhuart picking it for one of our 2018 panels at Phoenix Comic Fest to bring it to my attention. Thanks, dude!

I did, of course, know *Red Heat*, the film from which it takes its name as an overt pun. That was a buddy cop movie that mismatched brash Chicago detective Jim Belushi with visiting tough Russian police captain Arnold Schwarzenegger. The joy there, of course, is in figuring out how those two utterly different characters manage to find some common ground. Well here, our cops become about as different as could possibly be imagined: one of them quickly dies a horrible death but, through the central conceit of the movie, continues on in his job anyway. Suddenly, finding common ground really shouldn't be the object any more.

They're partners from moment one, wise-cracking detectives in the LAPD who aren't remotely on their captain's happy list, even after they stop the bad guys who murder a whole smörgåsbord of cops within the first five minutes of the feature. Here's the background: two crooks rob a jewellery store and take their own sweet time about it so, by the time they leave the building, what seems like half the LAPD is parked outside with guns locked and loaded, ready to take them down.

The ensuing firefight, however, is astoundingly one-sided in the other direction: cops die, in large numbers, but crooks don't. They bleed, sure, but they don't die, they don't move out of the immediate line of fire and they don't stop shooting until they run out of ammo. Why none of these cops goes for a head shot, I have no idea; maybe the LAPD don't use zombie flicks as training material. In the end, one perp bites it when his grenade explodes under him and the other when Roger Mortis uses him as the meat in a two car sandwich.

Yeah, Roger Mortis. That's a terrible pun of a name for a lead character who spends most of the movie dead but still walking around. He's played by Treat Williams, almost a decade after his first Golden Globe nod for starring in *Hair*, seven since his second for *Prince of the City*, in which he battled police corruption from the inside, and three since his third for *A Streetcar Named Desire*. His partner, at least, has a normal, if Hollywood, name, Doug Bigelow, and he's played by *Saturday Night Live* comedian, Joe Piscopo. His biggest film role thus far had been alongside Danny DeVito as one of a pair of lowest level mobsters on the run in Brian DePalma's comedy feature, *Wise Guys*.

The case at hand is the Cash and Dash gang, of whose exploits this is just the latest. There have been half a dozen robberies within two weeks: three banks, two jewellery stores and a goldsmith's shop. All the jobs have been pulled in broad daylight by heavily armed pairs of thieves, who don't die when they're shot. Clearly each of these jobs are connected, but it's

only now, with a pair of bodies in the morgue to examine, that Mortis and Bigelow start to break ground on the case.

And the breakthrough is a doozy! The coroner (and Roger's ex), Rebecca Smythers, quickly realises from the recognisable wounds on their chests that both men have been in the morgue before. In fact, they've already both been autopsied and she certified them dead personally. Yet, there they were that morning quite clearly mowing down cops in front of the watching TV cameras. She finds an obscure drug called sulfathiozole in each of their skin tissues, which Dante Pharmaceuticals recently bought in a notable large quantity. And so the investigation begins.

Naturally, Mortis and Bigelow go to Dante to ask about the drug and shake the metaphorical tree to see what falls out. While Randi James, the head of PR, gives them a tour of the premises, Bigelow sneaks off to break into a restricted area, wake up a grotesquely bloated resurrected corpse who looks like he has at least three faces stitched together and battle him at length. In the ensuing struggle with this monster, Mortis finds himself stuck inside the asphyxiation chamber in which Dante humanely destroys its obsolete test animals. An unknown hand switches on the device to suck out all the air and, well, as if his name was designed to be prophetic, that's all for him, folks.

Or is it? Given that the incident magically removes all Dante personnel from the entire building, as if it were staffed by invisible robots, Bigelow

shows Rebecca the space age laboratory where he woke the sleeping giant and she's fascinated. "This is how they do it," she tells him. "This is how they resurrect the dead." And, in a demonstration of IT so authentic that it would even have been rejected by *CSI: Miami*, she chats with the computer system in raw text and follows its instructions. She types in the details of how Mortis died and, hey, it's just dying to help. "Position body on table," it starts and, a few minutes later, after the requisite amount of artificial lightning, Detective Mortis opens his eyes and wonders what's up.

"It's great to be alive," he says. "I never felt better in my life." Except he has no heartbeat, he's cold and, when he oh so conveniently slits an artery by accident, he doesn't bleed. Oh, and that's not the worst of it, as Rebecca discovers remarkably quickly, given all the various circumstances. He has only ten to twelve hours, she tells him. Then his cells will degenerate into an organic stew and he'll be dead once more, but for good this time.

Now that we know this, the bad guys can start looking like the zombies that they really are. That wouldn't have been helpful at the beginning, of course, or we'd have figured all this out from moment one. Not that the movie's title and its tagline of "You can't keep a good cop dead" weren't dead giveaways, if you pardon the pun. It's just odd to see the filmmakers deal with plot inconveniences along with the growing collection of plot conveniences. Someone apparently said, "Hang on. We can't do that or..." and it's frankly rather a big surprise to me that they cared enough to do

so. And, in the preeminent question of the day, now that they've set that precedent, why didn't they do so more often?

What I've missed out thus far is the tone of the film. Sure, it's all about the resurrection of the dead, with a token nod to what we might do if we knew how long we had left to live, but this is a comedy more than it is a horror film, a sci-fi movie or an action flick and it's notably brutal with its jokes. The only people who can tell jokes this inappropriate in scenes this tough without an ounce of emotion are serial killers. Maybe Mortis is just used to his partner's sense of humour but, if I was their captain, I'd have Det. Bigelow in the psychiatrist's office to figure out if he's a sociopath.

For instance, Doug takes his partner's death and resurrection utterly in stride, but their next stop—visiting Randi James at home, because she ran out on the chaos at her workplace earlier—is interrupted by two zombies with machine guns. Our heroes win violently; Mortis takes one down by hiding underwater in the jacuzzi, body slamming his attacker in with him when he ventures near enough, then climbing out and throwing in a boom box to electrocute him. It's gruesome but Bigelow's reaction is calm. "You were underwater in that jacuzzi for five straight minutes," he tells Mortis. "Can you teach my girlfriend how to do that?"

Bigelow has so little empathy that I reckon he'd fail the Voight-Kampff test in under three questions, perhaps just one, so he could be a really bad replicant. Maybe that's why he's so fundamentally interested in enforced

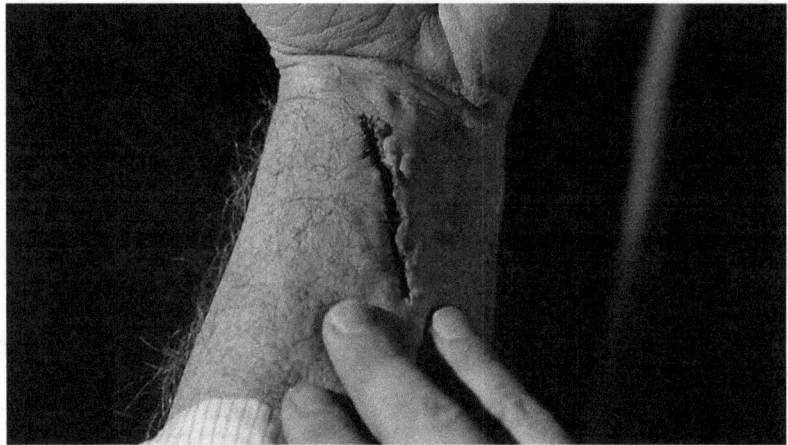

mortality and how much time we each have left. He's already talked about his ideas about deathday parties, in the morgue, no less, and, when Randi James first explains the function of the asphyxiation chamber to him, his response is to ask, "Didn't I see one of these at Disneyland?"

That's not to say there isn't imagination in play here; it's just not key to the progression of the story. For instance, we have a number of guest stars and we're about to meet a couple of them for a truly fantastic scene set in a Chinatown butcher's shop. The butcher is Professor Toru Tanaka, pro-wrestler turned actor, and his boss, Thule, is Keye Luke, perennial number one son to Charlie Chan and the original Kato in *The Green Hornet* serial in 1940, not to forget Master Po in *Kung Fu*. It's great to see both of them, but they vanish quickly, Thule after distracting our heroes by triggering a wild device that resurrects all the meat in the shop, from the headless corpse of a cow all the way down to individual slices and chunks of flesh. Bigelow, of course, is calm as a cucumber and becomes engrossed by a zombie duck head. "This could replace the whoopie cushion," he suggests.

The most obvious guest star, of course, is Vincent Price who, like Keye Luke, was closing in on the end of his long film career; each of them had three features left in filmographies that ran about a hundred pictures. He shows up here as a dying man on a videotape, Arthur P. Loudermilk, with a personal message for Randi James, his apparent daughter, whom he calls "princess". Dante Pharmaceuticals was his private think tank so, when we

discover that he died two weeks ago, we can immediately figure out much of where the script is going to take us. He may or may not have conquered death in *Dr. Phibes Rises Again*, but he certainly does here. So yes, he gets further scenes and he has a lot of fun with them but the tone of this film doesn't suit him, because it has no subtlety or elegance at all.

While the resurrection of Vincent Price isn't remotely surprising and the reveal of his chief accomplice is even less so, there are a few things that I didn't see coming at all, from twists in the tale to simple comments like Darren McGavin calling Vincent Price an old fart, which is priceless. Well, not quite, given that it inherently has a Price, but you know what I mean. What surprised me most of all, though, is how clever this script got at points where it didn't matter in the slightest, but couldn't be bothered when it did. The best line of the film is probably, "This could be the end of a beautiful friendship." Ah, appropriate homage, I've missed you! Yet, the majority of the dialogue is as fundamentally crass as, "I've seen meat loaf that looks better than you." I was surprised to find that this wasn't written by two different people with antagonistic approaches, but it's just Terry Black. Hey, maybe he's schizophrenic.

I'd classify *Dead Heat* as awesomely awful becauses it plays relatively poorly on a first viewing but doesn't go away. Maybe we see through the plot. Maybe we react negatively to the incessant sociopathic jokes. Maybe we wonder how the film could have been so much more, if it could just be

bothered. But, later, when we think about it, there's much that stands out, from the wild concept that's effectively a modern day *D.O.A.* in which a zombie cop has to solve his own murder—the original version of *D.O.A.* is playing on a television at one key moment in the film—to a host of little details here and there.

For instance, one of my favourite moments, albeit another sociopathic one when you analyse it, has Mortis locked in the back of an ambulance. He manages to nudge it into motion so that it rolls down the frickin' hill, to cause a deliberate and inevitable accident that will prompt people to come and investigate. When they do, he unzips his own body bag, borrows a gun and bike from a stunned cop and rides off to save the day. That's classic eighties cinema right there, a *Terminator* moment, and I love it.

Now, If I had to decide between *Red Heat* and *Dead Heat*, I'd go with the former but this one does things that that one could never have done, so it earned its status as a cult movie. Now, "how long have I got not to live?"

The Awesomely Awful '80s, Part 2

The Awesomely Awful '80s, Part 2

Hollywood Chainsaw Hookers

Director: Fred Olen Ray
Writers: Fred Olen Ray and T. L. Lankford, based on a screenplay by Dr. S. Carver and B. J. Nestles
Stars: Gunnar Hansen, Linnea Quigley, Jay Richardson, Dawn Wildsmith, Michelle McLellan, Dennis Mooney, Jerry Fox, Esther Alise, Tricia Burns, Jimmy Williams and Dukey Flyswatter

If the title of this movie left you in any doubt as to whether it would be awesomely awful, let me quote the introductory warning from Fred Olen Ray, the film's director and co-writer, verbatim:

"The CHAINSAWS used in this Motion Picture are REAL and DANGEROUS! They are handled here by seasoned PROFESSIONALS. The makers of this Motion Picture advise strongly against anyone attempting to perform these stunts at home. Especially if you are naked and about to engage in strenuous SEX."

That piqued your interest, huh? Well, it piqued the interest of the U.K. censors too, because they got their knickers in a twist over the inclusion of the word "chainsaw" in the title. So I first saw this under the title of *Hollywood Hookers* with a picture of a chainsaw in between the two words as a sort of sly wink at compliance. Hey, we didn't even get the *Teenage Mutant Ninja Turtles* in England, because those same censors imagined the hospital wards full of little kids who had put their eyes out playing with nunchucks and throwing stars. We got *Teenage Mutant Hero Turtles* instead.

Whatever the name it goes by—and *Hollywood Hookers* was at least closer to the original than the U.K. title for *Sorority Babes in the Slimeball Bowl-O-Rama*, another low budget 1988 picture featuring scream queens Linnea Quigley and Michelle Bauer, because that was inexplicably shortened to *The Imp*—this one is a whole bundle of fun, as its tongue is inserted firmly inside its cheek. For a great example, look no further than the very first death scene, in which "Boycott Britain" signs are prominent on Bauer's dresser, in rather quick response to the BBFC, those British censors.

Bauer, by the way, is one of those Hollywood chainsaw hookers of the title, Mercedes by name. She picks up some construction worker at a bar and takes him back to her place for some TFC (and I'll let you work that one out—this is a family friendly review of Hollywood Chainsaw Hookers). She gets him in the mood with a drink, drops the needle on some Elvis and drapes up transparent tarp over his portrait opposite the bed.

"Sometimes I get carried away," she explains, putting on a hairnet, which is far sexier than it sounds. Then, as he closes his eyes for Mama Mercedes, she whips out her special toy. "Take me to Heaven," he moans at her. "Your wish is my demand!" she replies, revving up her chainsaw. I should add that her aim is truly impeccable, given that the King would have been utterly drenched in gore by the time she finished if she hadn't have covered him up, but the rest of the room remains miraculously clean without a single drop of blood anywhere but the tarp.

Now, you might be wondering what sort of business plan these hookers have, because the chance of repeat clientele or referrals is pretty slim given the circumstances. In fact, you might be wondering about rather a lot of things here, you know, like why Hollywood, why hookers and why

frickin' chainsaws? Well, sit back and listen close, folk, because it all makes perfect sense. I promise.

Why Hollywood? Well, that's where all the pretty young things go, to find fame and fortune in America's Tinseltown. Why hookers? Because not all of those pretty young things make it and the pay's better than working at Taco Bell. And why chainsaws? Well, let's hold off on that answer until I've introduced you to Jack Chandler and Samantha Kelso.

Jack is a private detective and you can be sure that we're going to get dick jokes right up the wazoo. "Being a dick is a twenty-four hour a day job," he explains. Yeah, they milk that every chance they get. "Just what I need," mentions a cop. "A private dick in my face." Now, the humour isn't actually as puerile as this suggests because some of the bad puns to which we're exposed did have me nodding my head in respect, but hey, they are still bad puns. Oh, you want an example? How about this one: Jack thinks this whole chainsaw hooker debacle is a "love 'em and cleave 'em racket." Ha! In keeping with his profession, the whole tone of the movie is film noir and he's a really old school private dick, one with a permanent five o'clock shadow who drinks bourbon with a bourbon chaser and feels the need to narrate to us every few minutes just to keep us caught up.

Samantha is a runaway teenage beauty from Oxnard and Jack's current case. We know he's going to find her because she's sleeping on his couch

while he's knocking this story out on his manual typewriter. Well, typing something. I'd suggest it isn't this, because he clearly isn't touching the top row of letters and you can't get far without the letter "E", but then it does suddenly strike me that there isn't one in *Hollywood Chainsaw Hookers*.

Now, film noir detectives wouldn't have a job to do if the cops had done theirs first, so don't be too surprised to find some inept boys in blue here. Think modern day Keystone Kops without the slapstick. They're truly inept, even though they did arrest one of the chainsaw hookers. "The boys in interrogation screwed up big time," Captain Harrison explains to Jack. "They thought the sight of the murder weapon might shock her into spilling her guts. Only problem was they forgot to take the gas out of it and she spilled *their* guts instead." They are, at least, progressive enough to utilise innovative crime-fighting techniques such as including, "If you have committed a recent homicide, please stay on the line," on their++ answerphone message.

Of course, the police would probably be able to do a better job if private dicks didn't steal crucial evidence from their labs. Chandler is there when the techs examine a paper bag full of human fingers and, by instinct, he picks up the matchbook that was stuck to the bottom, which turns out to have Mercedes's phone number inside. One date with her and suddenly he finds himself tied to a bed while the story explains itself all around him. It

The Awesomely Awful '80s, Part 2

really is that much of a shortcut. Who was dancing topless on stage when he and Mercedes found a table? You have only one guess.

And here I can answer that last question—why chainsaws?—because the top billed actor finally gets round to speaking 37m into the frickin' movie. To be fair, he was cast here because the role that made him famous over a decade earlier also involved a chainsaw and, to the best of my recollection, he doesn't say a word in that entire feature, even though he's easily the most iconic thing in it. He's Gunnar Hansen, best known as Leatherface in Tobe Hooper's *The Texas Chain Saw Massacre*, and here he's... well, let's let Jack set that up for us. "What are you?" he asks the soft-spoken Hansen, who's credited only as "The Stranger" and looks rather like H. R. Giger in ceremonial garb. "The high priest character or something? What is this? Some ancient chainsaw worshipping cult?" The Stranger simply replies, "Actually, that's just what it is."

I'll let you ponder on that until you've had enough beers for it to make sense. I did mention that this film doesn't remotely take itself seriously, right? According to the opening credits, the screenplay was written by Dr. S. Carver and B. J. Nestles, but then "drastically rewritten and improved upon" by Fred Olen Ray and T. L. Lankford. I'd feel sorry for Dr. S. Carver if I didn't know that was Ray himself under a pseudonym. Then again, it had to be someone under a pseudonym!

What's weird is that this is alternately imaginatively clever, often in the gloriously dry monologues Jack delivers and in the priceless dialogue, and wildly inept at progressing a plot. I can't pass over the opportunity to quote Jack's narration when he proves unwittingly prescient about the state of the union here in 2018: "I'd stumbled into the middle of an evil, insidious cult of chainsaw worshipping maniacs," he ponders. "I had to wonder if we'd let our religious freedom go too far in this country or maybe our immigration laws were just too lax." And he thought he was just being funny. He was really being topical, thirty years too soon.

Yet, this film takes the art of plot convenience to new highs. Hopefully this book highlights how convenient the plots of awesomely awful movies of the eighties were in general, but this one is a step above every single one of them. For instance, I'm sure it won't be too surprising if I tell you that Jack does indeed escape from the bed to which he's tied and also, with the inevitable inside help, manages to wend his weary way to the finalé at the Stranger's Egyptian temple, but how does he do it?

Well, he drives around Los Angeles until he sees the signs. I'm serious. How about: "Temple This Way." Or: "Keep Going. You're Almost There." And: "Please Wait Until Your Number is Called." Now, that is objectively funny, I'll grant, but having a plot progression that makes sense really wouldn't have hurt the film.

A larger budget wouldn't have hurt the film either. I don't know how much they spent, because there are wildly different reports, but certainly it didn't make it to six figures. It's most obviously lacking in the temple, where Ray had to add a crowd applause track because the entire audience for Linnea Quigley's famous Virgin Dance of the Double Chainsaws is four bored hookers talking to each other. When the fit hits the shan and they all have to evacuate, they try to make the place look busier by running back and forth in front of the camera, as if we're not going to notice the same faces over and over again. Pattern recognition is a bitch.

But such are the trials and tribulations of low budget filmmakers. I'm not going to diss Fred Olen Ray, who has proved time and time again that he's able to get the job done. In fact, he's said in interviews that that's why he got jobs like this one: he kept demonstrating that he could bring in the films he was given on time and under budget. That was easily the most important attribute any director could have in the straight-to-video era and he kept that reputation going after the market changed and he found a similar prolificity in soft porn movies for cable television, under a whole string of pseudonyms, sadly none of which are puns.

I particularly liked his output in the eighties and early nineties, with a variety of films like *Inner Sanctum*, *Alienator* and *Wizards of the Demon Sword*, all of which I'm long overdue to revisit, once I find a PAL VCR to play them

again. It was he (along with Jim Wynorski, who made *Deathstalker II*) who created the infamous *Hollywood Scream Queen Hot Tub Party*, very likely the most honest exploitation picture ever made. Yeah, I have that on VHS too. Lately he's been on something of a bikini kick, for some reason, with titles like *Bikini Chain Gang*, *Bikini Girls from the Lost Planet* and *Ghost in a Teeny Bikini*. Clearly none of these are too likely to win a Golden Globe, but I bet they're fun and Fred Olen Ray brought them in on time and under budget.

Ray's career is clear evidence that time changes everything. I feel for the youth of today, with their streaming Netflix and their IMDb, who will never know the joys of perusing the spines of videocassettes on the shelf of a local mom and pop store to find the wildest titles, then trying to guess which of their fantastic covers might actually represent the low budget films inside the box. Those were the days when marketing was everything. The movies could suck royally as long as people kept on renting them and, yes, we would absolutely keep on renting movies like *Hollywood Chainsaw Hookers* because word of mouth ensured it. That's why we even rented *Hollywood* [silhouette of a chainsaw] *Hookers*. To hijack another of Gunnar Hansen's lines: "It's a very important part of our religion."

> The CHAINSAWS used in this Motion Picture are REAL and DANGEROUS! They are handled here by seasoned PROFESSIONALS. The makers of this Motion Picture advise strongly against anyone attempting to perform these stunts at home. Especially if you are naked and about to engage in strenuous SEX.
>
> My Conscience Is Clear
>
> Fred Olen Ray

The Awesomely Awful '80s, Part 2

The Awesomely Awful '80s, Part 2

Action Jackson

Director: Craig R. Baxley
Writer: Robert Reneau
Stars: Carl Weathers, Craig T. Nelson, Vanity, Sharon Stone, Thomas F. Wilson, Bill Duke, Robert Davi, Jack Thibeau, Roger Aaron Brown and Stan Foster

1988 was pretty late for a blaxploitation movie, but Carl Weathers—who had small roles in *Bucktown* and *Friday Foster* in between fame in American football and fame in *Rocky*—felt the need to conjure one up while shooting *Predator* a year earlier and he brought many of his fellow cast members along for the ride. Maybe they were the inspiration. Given that the script is hardly the film's best point and not every scene features an explosion, figuring out which eighties action movies you saw each of these guys in is a fun little game to play on the side.

There really is a lot of talent here, but it's not always the talent that you might expect and some of it is put to surprising use. For instance, this is a testosterone fuelled action movie, so the ladies don't really get much of a look-in, but this one does at least have more of them than *Bloodsport*. That had two; this has three (plus a hooker who gets a memorable scene in the 13th district police station).

The most obvious is Vanity, whom we last saw in *The Last Dragon*, where she seemed pretty good, even though her music sucked. Here, the music is a little better, but she's awful for most of the movie, as the drug-addled mistress of the chief bad guy who apparently wants to sleep with anyone who speaks to her. She landed a Razzie nomination for her work (she lost to Liza Minnelli for *Arthur 2: On the Rocks* and *Rent-a-Cop*) and that's fair for a change. How she suddenly turns into the romantic interest for our hero, Sgt. Jericho "Action" Jackson, I have no idea. Two days with him and she'll give up smack! Yeah, we believe you, Vanity. In real life, she was hooked on crack cocaine and it took an overdose, total renal failure and a personal visit from Jesus to get her past that. Are we to believe that a cop she's just met driving her down a back alley in a stolen black and white at eighty miles an hour trumps that? Somehow I don't think so.

The other is the villain's trophy second wife, played by Sharon Stone. She shows much more talent—and just as many boobs, because neither of these ladies had a non-nudity contract. It does seem rather wasteful of her talent to cast Stone as a topless corpse, but she was still building a career here and she does pretty well in the scenes before that. She was travelling through the usual cycle of extra work (*Stardust Memories*), horror movie (*Deadly Blessing*), wannabe blockbuster (*King Solomon's Mines*), outrageous and embarrassing misstep (*Police Academy 4: Citizens on Patrol*) and action flicks like this. A couple of years later she would land *Total Recall*; a couple more she would cross her legs in *Basic Instinct* and the rest is history. She isn't in this for long but, unlike Vanity, it's worth leaving on her resume.

So, with the ladies out of the way—the third and best is a cigar-chewing information source in a barber shop, a role that would usually be given to a man but here goes to the excellent Armelia McQueen—we can get down to exploring the flimsy plot.

Sgt. Jackson used to be Lt. Jackson but he got caught doing some of the things to Sean Dellaplane that we love watching cops do in eighties action

flicks but hate to see them do in real life. "You nearly tore that boy's arm off," complains Captain Armbruster; "He had a spare!" replies Jackson. Of course, the lieutenant's real mistake was in either not realising or not caring that the boy wasn't just a sexual psychopath, he was also the son of Peter Dellaplane, a man rich and powerful enough to run a car company in Detroit with his own name on it. And that's why he's now a sergeant.

We enter this story after two years, which Jackson has spent not only as a sergeant but without a gun permit or a wife, who left him when she felt his career was going in the wrong direction. Now he's being sent to watch Peter Dellaplane be honoured by the Detroit Businessman's League as Man of the Year. His captain wants to see if he can deal with that. He can, even though he tells everyone there what he thinks of the man, including, in a notable faux pas, his enemy's new wife. Really, it's just a way to introduce us to Peter Dellaplane so that we can understand that he's the bad guy. We haven't got far enough into the script to know what bad things he's doing but whatever they are, he's the one doing them. That neatly excises all the tedious mystery, ambiguity and character building that some films go for, instead settling for a virtual boxing match where Jackson and Dellaplane can just jab at each other for an hour and a half until the good guy wins.

Of course, these jabs aren't generally literal, though I should point out that our villain here is played by Craig T. Nelson, who was probably best

known at the time for a couple of *Poltergeist* movies because he wouldn't start his nine year run as *Coach* until the following year. That fluke of time may be the one and only reason why the eventual kickboxing showdown between Apollo Creed and Coach isn't immediately ludicrous. At least it's not quite up there with the Jackie Chan vs. Peter Fonda mismatch in *The Cannonball Run*, but it will take something spectacular to top that one!

While their jabs at each other mostly aren't literal, they're often wildly explosive. For instance, when Dellaplane's trophy wife leaves their house to talk with "Action" Jackson, she's deemed surplus to requirements and an employee is sent to run them both down with his yellow cab. Jackson saves the girl, of course, and gives chase. He's on foot but he keeps up with the taxi magnificently, eventually leaping onto its roof and punching out its windscreen. When he's finally thrown off and lands in front of the cab, he, honest to God, challenges it to a game of chicken. I lost track of how many cars have been destroyed thus far but he'll jump over the charging cab, so distracting its driver long enough for the vehicle to take off and fly into a car showroom. Now we know how Jackson got his nickname! Oh, and the driver escapes so rendering the entire chase scene non-productive but nobody ever mentions the multi-million dollar damage caused. Maybe destroying cars is a good thing in Detroit, because replacing them helps the local economy. I didn't check to see how many were Japanese.

The Awesomely Awful '80s, Part 2

One thing that impressed me, apart from the plethora of recognisable faces from action movies, was how this one doesn't always play it by the book. Sure, it might have the most eighties soundtrack ever, courtesy of both Michael Kamen and Herbie Hancock, with a couple of cheesy songs by Sister Sledge and the Pointer Sisters; I'd avoided all this at the time by virtue of being too busy stagediving to Napalm Death. But it seems to like flouting the rules that had gradually coalesced around what has to happen in eighties action movies.

For example, let me introduce you to the two cops we meet early on in the movie and who are then unfortunately sidelined for most of the rest of it. They're Officers Lack and Kornblau and they have a glorious time with a not-too-bright small time opportunist thief called Albert Smith. "This kid would have to go to college for four years just to reach the level of shit for brains," points out Lack, who's willing to use mild profanity even though he enunciates magnificently and is happy to use the word "ne'er-do-well" to describe the moron. Unsurprisingly, Lack is played by a Shakespearean actor, Roger Aaron Brown. More surprisingly, he's the African American half of the partnership and that's just the first refreshing aspect to them.

We catch up with them catching up with him. He's stupid enough to attempt to steal a lady's purse right in front of them, but they don't do any of the requisite shouting and posturing; they merely wait for the large

black lady (clearly a stuntman in drag) to stop beating him with her purse before taking him downtown. In the car, they scare the wits out of the poor boy by regaling him with tall tales about "Action" Jackson, every one of which he buys hook, line and sinker, but it's refreshingly done because they're the opposite of bullies: polite, well-spoken and courteous. Oh, and Kornblau is played by Thomas F. Wilson, who you know as Biff Tannen.

Really, this whole section is just a slow build to introduce us to Jackson. Our polite cops get poor Albert to the station, but he's so scared by their stories that he runs the first moment he gets, colliding into everyone and everything, eventually crashing into a random desk and covering it and its contents with hot coffee. He looks up to see the nameplate, then further to see the man standing up behind it and faints clean away when Sgt. Jackson says, "Mellow out." Hilariously, if you pay attention, he sees him again a couple of scenes later through a few glass windows, and faints once more.

So we've met our hero and we've met our villain. All we need now is the reason why they're going to go at it and that's a pretty transparent one. The dead bodies piling up are all prominent officials of the A.W.A. or Auto Workers Alliance, an automobile industry union, and Dellaplane runs a car company. I'm not sure we have any more than two dots that need to be connected here. The film was rated R but the plot could have been rated K for Kindergarten. Of course, the authorities don't acknowledge that and so

The Awesomely Awful '80s, Part 2

focus on Jackson himself, as the sole suspect in the murder of Dellaplane's trophy wife. Yeah, the villain is so villainous that he shoots his own wife dead during a loving clinch, even though she's played by the delectable Sharon Stone.

Really, the plot doesn't matter because it's just something for the story to improvise around as writer Robert Reneau figures out how to make an hour and a half seem interesting until we get to the boss battle. He tries a few things, including having Vanity play a singer, Sydney Ash, so that she can sing a couple of tunes without it seeming out of place. However, only two of these approaches really work.

One is spectacular death scenes, especially early on, which highlight the capability of the stunt team and the cinematographer. Frank Stringer dies before the opening credits, after a set of invaders rapel down from the roof and crash into his penthouse apartment; after a little to and fro, they blow him right out of it to flail down to ground level on fire, neatly shot from below. There are a lot of fire stunts here and they're done very well indeed. The second death is Lionel Grantham, who's listening to opera on his yacht; the same team come aboard and handcuff a bomb to his wrist with less than ten seconds on the clock. The cameras withdraw to a safe distance and the subsequent screen-filling explosion neatly illuminates the killers escaping by dinghy. The explosions are done very well too.

The other is pointless side scenes that add in those recognisable faces. For instance, at one point, we follow Jackson and Sydney Ash to a pool hall so that he can talk to someone we've never heard of for reasons that don't matter. It turns out that he's dead, which isn't important. What matters is that his balls are being kept in a jar in a back room closet and the people who took them want to add Jackson's to the collection. Why? No reason. They could have just pointed out that, "Sorry, man, he died last year," and that would have been the end of it, but that wouldn't have given some actors enough to do and, frankly, that's the real point of the scene.

The bartender at this pool hall is a fantastic example. You'll recognise his face immediately but you'll try to figure out why and you won't have a name to go on. Just because I'm a nice guy, I'll help you out. He's Charles Meshack and he's the character who gets Arnie onto a plane in *Commando*. You know, the one he tells the stewardess not to disturb because, "He's dead tired." The gentleman who tries to take Jackson's balls is another great example. He's Branscombe Richard, perhaps best known as Bobby Sixkiller in *Renegade*, but you may well recognise him from *Commando* too.

There are so many of these that it sometimes feels like every actor who ever spoke in a Schwarzenegger movie got a role here, but in reality it's just all the male non-Caucasians. You won't see Jesse Ventura, Sven-Ole Thorsen or Vernon Wells here and you won't see Rae Dawn Chong, but

The Awesomely Awful '80s, Part 2

you'll see pretty much everyone else. You're probably thinking about the Native American from *Predator* right now. Yeah, he's here too as a sweary drug dealer. Some of them even did more than one, like Bill Duke, who was in both *Predator* and *Commando* and plays Jackson's captain here.

I counted at least five members of the *Die Hard* cast too, not the major ones but still ones you'll recognise anyway, like De'voreaux White, who played John McClane's limo driver, Argyle, and Al Leong, who's surely the most recognisable heavy in Hollywood, the first on the cast list if they ever make a Chinese spaghetti western. It's even odds whether you know him best from *Big Trouble in Little China* or *Lethal Weapon*. I'm just shocked that he didn't make it into an Arnie film until *Last Action Hero* in 1993. Oh, and our opening victim here, played by Robert Davi, was in *Die Hard* but supported Arnie in *Raw Deal*; however, you'll probably know him best as the opera singing bad guy in *The Goonies*.

And trust me, I've just scraped the surface. You'll find a whole bunch more yourselves, while you're not listening to Vanity sing and you're not watching this plot fail to develop. I think Carl Weathers wanted this film to happen so badly that he promised everyone he'd ever worked with, the actors and the stuntmen and the folk serving lunch, roles in it if they just mentioned how great it would be when they were in the elevator with the studio boss. I'm guessing that's how this got made. The standard story is

that he discovered a shared love of blaxploitation films with producer Joel Silver, while making *Predator*, but that seems far too easy for something this fundamentally broken.

The Awesomely Awful '80s, Part 2

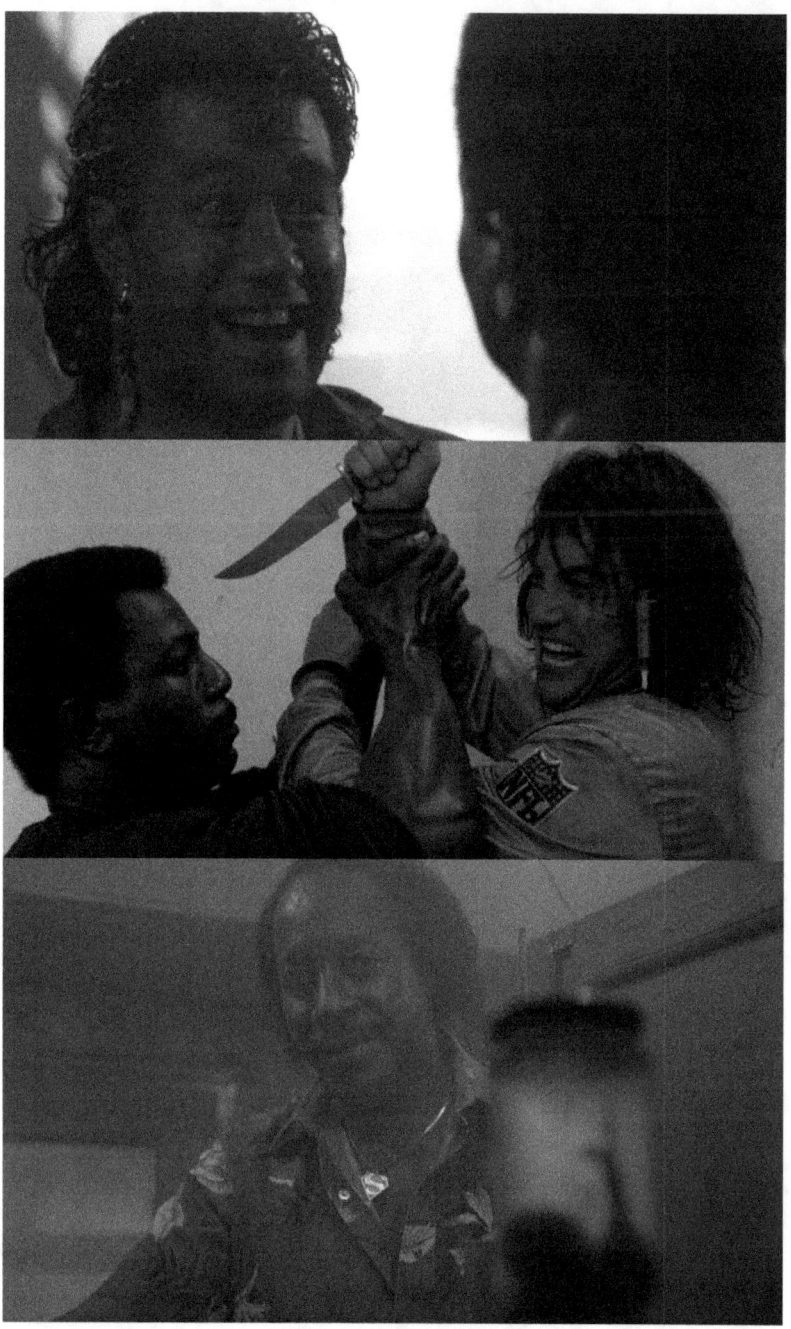

The Awesomely Awful '80s, Part 2

1989

The Horror Show
The Wizard
Robot Jox
See No Evil, Hear No Evil
Road House

The Horror Show

Director: James Isaac
Writers: Alan Smithee and Leslie Bohem
Stars: Lance Henriksen, Brion James, Rita Taggert, Dedee Pfeiffer, Aron Eisenberg, Thom Bray and Matt Clark

How good must a movie be if a director as great as David Blyth, who had already made *Death Warmed Up* and would go on to the superb *Wound*, can't do it justice? No, that's both wishful and backward thinking. Let's try that question again! How *bad* must be a movie be if a director as good as David Blyth gets fired partway through the shoot and one of the two writers, Allyn Warner, has his name switched to Alan Smithee, the standard credit for anyone who doesn't want anything to do with the movie they made?

Yeah, this one somehow ended up with a reputation as a turkey, with many critics focusing in on a particular scene where the villain manifests his taunting head on a turkey as somehow representative of the picture as a whole. We critics do have a habit of doing things like that, because we're lazy buggers at heart and that's an easy way to get a cheap laugh. Well, we critics should also be willing to go against the grain and fight for films (or against them) on their merits rather than what everyone else says. And I'll fight for this, which suffered from a number of awkward circumstances.

One is that the film was promoted outside the U.S. as part of the *House* series, to which it's connected only by a few crew members, under the titles of *House III: The Horror Show* or *Horror House: House III*. So, much of the film is set in a house? That must be almost every non-western feature out there, right? Well, apparently that's all the distributors needed, so now it serves mostly to confuse people looking backwards at that series, just like the otherwise excellent *Halloween III: Season of the Witch*, which simply has nothing to do with any of the other ~~nine~~ ten *Halloween* movies.

Don't even get me started on what the Italians did! Over there, the first couple of *Evil Dead* movies were called *La Casa* and *La Casa 2*, because, hey, they were partly set in a house (maybe the Italians don't have words for "cabin in the woods"). Then they made a bunch of unofficial sequels to be *La Casa 3, 4* and *5*, by which time the *House* movies had come along. What else are you going to call a movie called *House* in Italy but *La Casa*? So, they just kept upping the number. Oddly, *House* itself got left out, so *La Casa 6* is *House II: The Second Story* and this one, which shouldn't have been *House III* to begin with, got to be the even more inappropriate *La Casa 7*!

Adding to the confusion is the fact that the eighties were the heyday of "twin films", two notably similar movies released at the same time. No, not a mainstream film and a cheap "mockbuster" like the Asylum tends to contribute today but a pair of unrelated movies that happen to be alike, sourced from simple coincidence or maybe something in the Hollywood water. For every *Turner and Hooch*, there was a *K-9*. For every *Gremlins*, there was a *Ghoulies*. For every *Like Father, Like Son*, there was a *Big*, an *18 Again!* and a *Vice Versa*. Well, *The Horror Show* was followed very quickly by *Shocker* and the two are often mistaken in hindsight, not least by people suggesting that this one ripped off that one when it was actually released seven months earlier. Remember what I said about lazy critics? Many of them prefer Wes Craven's movie, but I'm rather partial to this one, not least because it stars Lance Henriksen and Brion James, two of the most underrated character actors in the genre. James has said that the role he

plays here, of mass murderer Max Jenke, was his personal favourite.

Jenke is a real piece of work. His nickname of "Meat Cleaver Max" is rather descriptive of what he gets up to in his spare time, but he's not just your average, run of the mill serial killer; he'd be a strong candidate for Olympic gold if the Americans got their national pastime added to the event roster. He was responsible for at least a hundred and ten victims, we're told, seven of whom were cops. And he leaves Det. Lucas McCarthy, the cop who finally brought him in, with recurring nightmares so bad that he feels he has to see Jenke executed in order to find peace.

That quickly turns out to be a terrible idea because pretty it isn't. Jenke is unrelenting: he spits his communion wafer back at the priest; his last words are profanity, directed at no less a warden than Lawrence Tierney, not someone you'd want to swear at under any other circumstances; and his final request is even to be buried with his treasured meat cleaver. In lesser hands, all this would be annoyingly cheesy, but this is Brion James we're talking about here. His electrocution scene is a real peach, because the electrocution part doesn't initially work. The warden has to call for more voltage, but Jenke hilariously echoes his plea. "Yeah, increase the voltage, shithead!" By the time he breaks out of the electric chair, burning alive, to swear to McCarthy that he's coming back for him, then he and we both had better take note. I'm just glad this wasn't shot in smell-o-vision!

That scene alone makes *The Horror Show* worthy for an awesomely awful

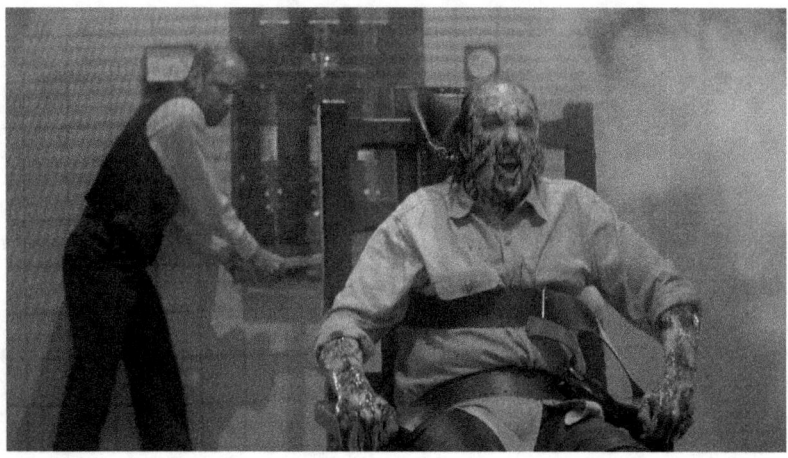

tag. But, because this is an eighties horror movie, of course he comes back. His spirit flits out of his body, which is lying in the morgue, in front of a university professor, Peter Campbell, who apparently has theories on this sort of phenomena and full permission to research them, and Max takes up residence in the furnace in McCarthy's basement. Because, you know, he could. From that point on, he has an absolute blast messing around with his captor's mind, appearing at every single inappropriate moment, manipulating reality and threatening violence with a high pitched cackle. It's toned down from the one in *Crimewave* but, yes, it's still there.

The biggest problem the film has is consistency, because there are two completely different approaches duelling for supremacy like teenagers in a *Pokémon* battle. Come to think of it, that would be a pretty cool game. "Max Jenke, I choose you!" It wouldn't surprise me if the writers had a difference of opinion on which approach was appropriate and that's why we ended up with an Alan Smithee credit.

The one that probably has all the critics rolling their eyes is the literal approach, the one in which Jenke does survive death by shifting out of our plane of existence and haunting McCarthy's house like a squatter ghost. It really doesn't make a whole heck of a lot of sense, even if we expound it in the voice of Prof. Peter Campbell of Columbia University. In fact, it makes even less sense when expounded in this voice of apparent experience, as it's a) totally nuts and b) something we completely forgot about because

Campbell vanishes from the film after the electrocution and doesn't show back up until we're a full hour in.

Anyway, let's suppress the chuckles and ask him what his research at such a respectable institute as Columbia happens to be. Ah yes, "pure evil as a form of electronic energy, an electricity of evil." I can totally see the dean signing off on his project grants based on that description! And, of course, Max Jenke was the most evil of the many evil psycho nutjobs (just check out his stats), so he must become the proof to Campbell's theories. Suddenly we wonder if those cackles are Brion James trying to be a scarier Freddy Kreuger or Thom Bray's subconscious mad scientist thinking about going completely batshit insane.

Now, we are given material that might support Campbell's arguments. For instance, he explains this theory to McCarthy while he's sitting in the electric chair in Jenke's apartment. That's right! This nutjob actually built his own home made electric chair to build up his immunity to the juice. But let's just think about this for a moment. Is everything we're watching part of his dastardly plan? Did he plan to be caught, specifically by Det. McCarthy, over whom he obsessed, after reaching a nice round kill score of "over one hundred and ten"? Did he plan to be fried in the electric chair, awkwardly and painfully? And did he then plan to transform into a spirit form of pure evil to be transmitted wirelessly through the ether using, I don't know, Bluetooth for Wackos® or some such protocol, to a

The Awesomely Awful '80s, Part 2

basement where he's going to live on in a frickin' furnace?

Why? He's out there having a blast a-slashin' and a-rapin' or whatever his personal fetishes are and a-runnin' the cops a-ragged. We can tell he's enjoying himself from little touches like placing the severed head of a cop on a kitchen plate and labelling it "Blue Plate Special". Surely the number one item on the master plan of someone who gets his kicks this way is to be able to keep on doing it. How about plan to not get frickin' caught? I'm sorry, but doesn't that make more sense? No wonder those critics thought this was a piece of crap. If that's how we're supposed to read this movie, I would heartily agree, especially as we get zero background on Jenke. Even at the point this movie ends, all we know about him is that he killed a lot of people with a meat cleaver. That's it. Oh, and he cackled while doing so.

So much for the literal approach. I'm happier with a psychological take on things, which may be a heck of a lot more confusing but I feel is much more rewarding in the long run. And we all want to be rewarded, don't we. Here, have a cookie. You didn't even have to take Prof. Campbell's class for that one, but hey, maybe Jenke did! How else would this wacko nutjob learn anything about the "electricity of evil"? A YouTube tutorial? By the way, I searched YouTube for "electricity of evil" because critics should do their homework and I learned how to turn the power on in the videogame *Black Ops III: Zombies*. So much for research. PS: Lucifer is electricity.

Personally, I'm a fan of the psychological approach here and feel that

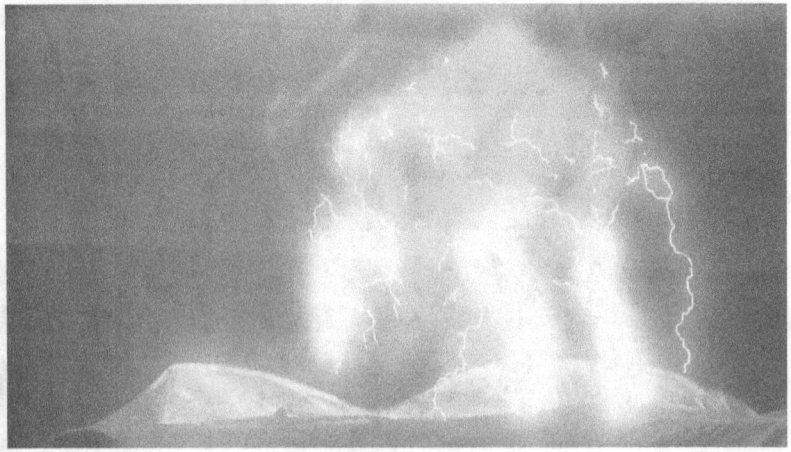

the film works pretty well from this standpoint. Only McCarthy himself notices their new unwelcome guest for a while and this makes him look as crazy as he starts to feel, stabbing the turkey when it grows Jenke's head on the side of its own or shooting the TV when Jenke takes over the role of a stand up comedian on the screen. "Take my wife... and disembowel her."

This approach means that when daughter Bonnie brings her boyfriend Vinnie home against explicit orders (hey, she'll be eighteen on Saturday!) and Jenke takes his cleaver to him, it's McCarthy who becomes the prime suspect, especially as the kids overhear him down there in the basement shouting at the furnace to leave his family alone when Bonnie's trying to find out where Vinnie has vanished to.

Given that McCarthy had almost strangled his wife in a nightmare even before Jenke is put into the electric chair and given that he's not going to be going back on duty until his psychiatrist signs off on his state of mind, we can assume that there are some mental issues here. Maybe everything is unfolding in his mind and the whole reincarnated evil spirit thing is just him stuck in a nightmarish attack of post-traumatic stress disorder. How brutal is it when the very people he's trying to protect start to wonder if he might actually be the one who's hurting them?

After all, McCarthy was on the Jenke case from the beginning. Cops know they can't save 'em all but they can try and, when they fail, they can fight the guilt that sits in their world like a kidney stone. Well, Jenke killed

more people than any other American serial killer—for anyone who cares, the real record currently sits with Gary Ridgway, the Green River Killer, who confessed to 71 victims and was convicted of 49; Jenke makes him look like an amateur. How must that count hurt McCarthy's conscience? Sure, he took him down in the end, but he was over a hundred and ten victims too late. That's unimaginably tough.

Personally, I'm happy to read this film as unfolding in McCarthy's mind as he tries to find a way to exorcise Jenke and the various demons that come with him so that he can go back to his job and not worry about hurting his family. In fact, that's the only way I can read it because I'm not going to base my interpretation on one wishy washy scene two thirds of the way through the movie when a character we'd forgotten about tries to sell us on wirelessly transmitted pure evil. For me, the biggest discussion point is in just how much (or how little) of this film is real.

Given the finalé, which features as uncharacteristally happy an ending as I've ever seen in a slasher movie, we can assume that much of the third act is imaginary. Maybe he never gets arrested for Vinnie's murder. Maybe Vinnie never gets murdered. Arguably, we could go all the way back to Jenke's electrocution or even further still. I could buy into McCarthy never actually leaving his psychiatrist's office, meaning that the entire picture takes place inside his head while he's being treated.

So, most critics see this movie as awful. I've never bought into that view

The Awesomely Awful '80s, Part 2

and I'm honestly starting to see it as awesome. For now, let's just split the difference and go with awesomely awful.

The Awesomely Awful '80s, Part 2

The Wizard

Director: Todd Holland
Writer: David Chisholm
Stars: Fred Savage, Christian Slater, Jenny Lewis, Luke Edwards, Will Seltzer, Sam McMurray, Frank McRae, Wendy Phillips, Jackey Vinson and Beau Bridges

Around the time this film was made, my favourite actor was undeniably Christian Slater. I'd love to talk about *Heathers*, *Gleaming the Cube* and *Pump Up the Volume*, all of which were made within a year of this picture, but they're simply too good to fit into an Awesomely Awful book. *The Wizard*, on the other hand, wouldn't fit anywhere else. Half Nintendo commercial and half *Rain Man* for kids, it's a truly awful film by any standards, but it does enough somehow to become a guilty pleasure.

Maybe it's the wish fulfilment angle. After all, Mr. Putnam, who rescues lost children for a living, a praiseworthy career which he manages to turn into something utterly seedy, spends most of the film wishing ill on Fred Savage and, as much as we would never be on the side of such an asshole mercenary psychopath, we're... well, we find ourselves on his side far too often. Now, I should add that the wish fulfilment angle that writer David Chisholm was actually going for is something rather different. His goal, I assume, was to place us on the side of the three kids who spend the entire film traumatising their parents by running away from home so they can play videogames in California. Yeah, he has to work hard at this one.

To be fair, it's not quite that simple and that's why we have a story. And it all begins with little Jimmy Woods—actor Luke Edwards was nine at the time—who begins the picture wandering down a soon to be dark desert highway to California with only a lunchbox for company. We're not given a reason yet so we can only assume that it was the warm smell of colitas, whatever they are[1], rising up through the air, but the shimmering light he sees up ahead in the distance turns out to be the plane out searching for him and the Fairleigh County sheriff promptly takes him back to his mum.

I would be failing in my duty if I didn't highlight that we are given a reason right at the end of the movie and I'm not ashamed to say that it's a really touching reason that will absolutely get you right there, unless your heart is made of iron, but nothing exists in this movie to get us from here to there, so I guess we're supposed to ignore it for now. Watching a second time does highlight a little telegraphing, especially in one scene almost halfway through, but it's nothing you'll be able to figure out in isolation.

I should also add that that this is a weird approach to take, given that that reason also prompts most of the rest of the drama that underpins this story. Like the fact that Jimmy's taken back to his mother, Christine, as his parents have divorced and she's moved on to marry a complete asshole (I have to emphasise here that I really don't use that word often, even after fourteen years in the U.S., but it does seem to be appropriate rather often in *The Wizard*). And the fact that his dad, Sam, has a poor relationship with his other sons, Corey and Nick. In fact, this reason explains so much of what we see that it's a little odd to find that we're not actually let in on the secret for far too long. You'd think they'd start with it, but hey.

Anyway, Jimmy has issues. I initially thought that he placed somewhere on the autistic spectrum, high functioning but with odd little habits that nobody else can explain that still clearly make sense to him. He's been in

some sort of therapeutic environment for a couple of years but it hasn't helped and the new husband decides that Jimmy will be much better off in an institution. So that's it for the poor little sod, who will now rot inside and his reason, whatever it might be, will die forgotten with him.

Well, not if his half-brother, Corey, has anything to say about it. He's a kid himself—actor Fred Savage was thirteen and already a star, courtesy of *The Princess Bride*, *Vice Versa* and *The Wonder Years*—but he's getting rather fed up of his dysfunctional family. Dad doesn't do anything, though mum won't let him, and his stepdad's an asshole. Even his elder brother, Nick, only cares about himself. So, with home life sucking royally, Corey takes matters into his own hands. He catches the bus downtown, slips into the institution in Green River, UT and breaks out his half-brother so he can take him to California. Why, he has no idea, but it's what Jimmy wants.

Now, Corey does prepare for this trip. He has a backpack and a map and a skateboard and presumably some water, something that Jimmy certainly didn't have on his walk into the desert. Unfortunately, he doesn't prepare very well because, hey, he's thirteen, and he's rather shocked to find that two bus tickets to California from some town outside Goblin Valley—"why not Axe Murderer's Valley?" he ponders—will be over a couple of hundred bucks. He has a sum total of $27.30. "What does that get us?" he asks the clerk. "Nowhere," comes the official reply.

What we discover next is that, as dysfunctional as this family is, they do

still care. The remaining Woods, Sam and Nick, jump in their pickup truck —which still has a tree in the back because Sam is a landscaper—and head out to find the kids, stopping everywhere and asking everyone questions. They'll track them down, however long it might take, because that's what family does. The Batemans, Christine and her unnamed husband, don't care enough to do it themselves; instead they hire Mr. Putnam. But only to find Jimmy. "Well, Corey wants to run away," they say. Screw him.

See what I mean about the word "asshole"? Bateman's working hard to be an asshole but Putnam's already a professional. He honestly warns off Sam Woods, Jimmy's father, as he won't get paid if someone else finds him first. When they end up in the same town, he slashes their tyres so as to gain an advantage; the ensuing grudge match between the two is as oddly funny as it is completely inappropriate. And, get this, the line he tries on a lady at his very first stop is, "Hey, sweetheart, I'm looking for some kids." Oh yeah, that should work fine! Nobody could possibly misinterpret that!

There's one more key character to introduce, as it's pretty clear that Corey and Jimmy aren't going to get too far on their own. And by not too far, I mean not out of the first town they somehow manage to reach. She's Haley, she's about Corey's age—actress Jenny Lewis was also thirteen—and she's from Reno. Her dad's a trucker, she says, who does a weekly run to Kansas City, and so she's streetsmart enough to help them find rides and make some money in between by hustling suckers on arcade machines. It's

The Awesomely Awful '80s, Part 2

Haley who even figures out where they need to go: Universal Studios for the Video Armageddon gaming tournament, sponsored by Nintendo.

I'm sure you're wondering at this point why she would be so specific. It has to be said that she's known Jimmy for less than a day and he's spoken precisely one word in that entire time, so she hardly knows him. However, while Corey was failing miserably at buying bus tickets to California and she was watching his reaction when a cop drives up, Jimmy was racking up a crazy score on *Double Dragon*. Corey's certainly amazed at his 50,000 point tally and he hadn't even finished his game. Then again, Corey thinks $27.30 is a vast sum of money and it'll sustain two on a trip to California, so what the heck does he know? Anyway, when Jimmy shows that he can play *Ninja Gaiden* too on a tabletop game in a café, clearly he's the wizard of the title and he'll win the $50,000 grand prize at Video Armageddon.

Yeah, you have to love the realism of children! Let's think about this for a moment. A thirteen year old kid kidnaps his mentally challenged nine year old half-brother and starts him on an out-of-state road trip for which they're woefully under-financed—entry into Universal Studios in 1989 was $15.50 per child so, even if a sparkly unicorn magically teleported them in an instant to the very gates of the event, Corey's $27.30 still wouldn't have got them in. They team up with a thirteen year old girl they find in a bus depot, without asking why she's ten hours from home and apparently wandering around the southwest for fun. Together, they'll find their way

to Universal City so this nine year old wizard can win them fifty grand in a tournament they know nothing about. Hey, it is more realistic than *Armageddon* and *Independence Day* put together. And yes, it's still a better love story than *Twilight*.

The thing is that wish fulfilment is a pretty powerful tool for kids and, if I'd have been young enough in 1989, I'd have probably been on their side, rooting for young Jimmy as he battles the asshole kid and the token girl in the Video Armaggedon finals. C'mon, you're surprised at that? Next thing, you'll be telling me that you'd be surprised when our heroic trio bump into that very same asshole kid on the journey there and his mad skills with a powerglove etch the first chink in Jimmy's previously invincible armour. Yeah, that happens too. There's very little that's surprising here.

Let's see. What's actually surprising?

Fred Savage's being the only name before the title is surprising. So his dad is Beau Bridges and his brother's Christian Slater? Who cares? This is a Fred Savage movie, even though it's Luke Edwards portraying the wizard of the title. Tobey Maguire, of *Spider-Man* fame, is surprising, just for the fact that he's here; he makes his film debut outside Video Armageddon as one of the asshole kid's hangers-on. I guess the fact that this picture isn't called *Nintendo: The Movie* is pretty surprising. We see games being played throughout the film, even before the $50,000 showdown; each and every one of them is a Nintendo game. They were the entire industry in 1989, if

this movie is anything to go on.

By the way, in the most outrageous example of product placement the film has to offer, that showdown even introduced the U.S. to a brand new Nintendo game a couple of months before its Stateside release. Talk about film as advertising! That game is *Super Mario Bros. 3* and it would become the third best-selling NES game of all time, not to mention its very own cartoon, *The Adventures of Super Mario Bros. 3*. This was part of a marketing blitz by Peter Main, a vice president at Nintendo of America, who brought the company to an 80% market share in 1989 selling $2.7 billion of product that year alone. The *New York Times* called him "Nintendo's Wizard".

Frankly, it's the tie to real life that makes this picture so interesting in hindsight. For instance, the introduction of the asshole kid, whose name is Lucas, prompts our heroes to do their homework on the Nintendo suite of games, which means we get to experience the Nintendo helpdesk along with them. Yes, that was a real thing! In case you got stuck on a game, you could ring a hotline and one of 120 game counselors would help you out.

My favourite section was another behind the scenes one, at Universal Studios in Universal City, CA. The various people searching for the kids do catch up with them, of course, in the break before the Video Armageddon final, because timing is everything. That prompts a glorious chase through the park, part of which is spent around the *King Kong* ride: on it, under it, behind it. I'm not much of a theme park fan, but I do find the mechanics

behind them fascinating and I had a lot of fun on the *King Kong* ride when I first visited Universal Studios in Florida.

The location at the end is a real one too, the one with the dinosaurs. It's at Cabazon, CA, just west of Palm Springs on I-10. Mr. Rex, the 65 foot tall tyrannosaurus rex, has been there since 1986 and Dinny the brontosaurus is over a decade older. I've been here, not because it was featured in *The Wizard* or *Pee-wee's Big Adventure* or a number of other films, TV shows and music videos, but because who can drive past dinosaurs without stopping? After the death of its founder, Claude Bell, in 1988, and its later sale by his family, it became a creationist museum. It's still a fun place, though, just one where you can't read the merchandise without laughing.

And that's good, because there's not a lot of laughter in *The Wizard*. It's a terrible movie but a fascinating time capsule, wrapped up in a drama that doesn't seem remotely important, either to us or the filmmakers, until the end when they turn up the movie magic and make us melt. Perhaps this was inevitable. After all, in better hands, this could have been a powerful drama, but then it wouldn't have been a 100m Nintendo commercial. Remove that aspect and it would become an utterly different picture that we wouldn't be watching thirty years later.

Frankly, it's only because it's a slice of life that we're still watching. It's cheesy, it's predictable and it's indefensible on so many levels (hey, I just made another pun and only noticed it while proofing). But it's a reminder

of a moment when Fred Savage was a megastar, Nintendo was everywhere and, if you made it through *Ninja Gaiden* without losing a life, you were a god. And if the eighties ever taught us anything, Ray, it was that "when someone asks you if you're a god, you say yes!"

[1] OK, I googled "colitas". It turns out that "cola" is the Spanish word for an animal's tail and "foxtails" is one of the many colloquial terms used to describe marijuana buds. So "colitas" apparently means weed, which is far less surprising than it ought to be. However, "cola" is also a slang term in Hispanic culture for "buttocks", so perhaps what the Eagles really smelled back in 1976 was just ass. Especially if they were drinking cola at the time.

Robot Jox

Director: Stuart Gordon
Writer: Joe Haldeman, based on a story by Stuart Gordon
Stars: Gary Graham, Anne-Marie Johnson, Paul Koslo, Robert Sampson, Danny Kamekona, Hilary Mason and Michael Alldredge

If you felt that *The Wizard* was unbelievable, then you're likely to have some issues with this, in some twisted ways its grown up cousin: Nintendo as the means for violent diplomacy in the post-apocalypse.

We're in the future, fifty years after a nuclear holocaust has wiped out most of the human race. Like *Hell Comes to Frogtown*, conflict continues but, unlike *Hell Comes to Frogtown*, it has nothing to do with enlisting men with high sperm counts and having them replenish the army by knocking up as many fertile women as can be found. Well, actually it does, but that's not our focus. There are adverts all over the place for pregnancy aids and being knocked up is seen as an honorable function for a woman. I do have to say that it's truly surreal to see Don Jackson and multi-award winning science fiction author Joe Haldeman working from the same page!

What's different is that Haldeman was cutting down for Lent on mutant reservations with races of mutant frog people dancing in radioactive bars. Instead he postulated a replacement for war, which is entirely outlawed in this future. All territorial disputes are now settled like gentlemen, having one man from either side suit up in a giant killing machine to batter each other to death. It's quite an attractive concept: a mecha duel featuring the people's champions. Who needs chemical weapons in Syria when we could end that civil war by having America's darling, Caitlyn Jenner, stomp Russia's Donald Trump in a one on one giant mecha battle?

I do love this futuristic take on an eternal concept, simplifying nations down to individuals, as we do every four years at the Olympics, just with a lot more riding on the competition than a mere gold medal. The good old

The Awesomely Awful '80s, Part 2

Roman fight to the death is honoured in the picture's French title of *Les gladiateurs de l'apocalypse* or, you know, *The Gladiators of the Apocalypse*. The Germans, naturally, went with a literal approach instead, *Die Schlacht der Stahlgiganten!* translating as *The Battle of the Steel Giants*. I'd dearly love to know what the Japanese called this film but they'd have been confused at the glaring lack of kawaii schoolgirls in the giant mecha movie so maybe it didn't play well there.

We come in at a crucial point, with Alexander winning somewhere for the Confederation at their Playing Ground in Siberia by literally crushing Hercules, the representative of the Market. That's nine victories in a row for Alexander and he's killed every one of his opponents thus far. As robot jox only get to fight ten times, he's about to retire with a perfect record, with only Achilles standing in his way. The thing is that Achilles has won his last nine fights too, so someone's surely going to fail at the last hurdle and we know exactly whose side we're all on.

You see, even though times they were a-changin' and the Berlin Wall was about to fall, *Robot Jox* is very much a product of the Cold War, albeit one it fictionally heated back up again. The Confederation are clearly the Soviets and Alexander is the stereotypical Russian machine, even though Paul Koslo, who overplays his part outrageously, wasn't Russian; casting a German born Canadian as a Soviet asshole who sounds like Tommy Wiseau was a touch of genius. The Market is just as clearly the west, though we

have no idea how much of it is left after that nuclear war, and Achilles is a red blooded all-American boy, played by Gary Graham, who was about to land his most famous role as Det. Matthew Sikes in *Alien Nation*.

Just in case that isn't enough for us to pick our side, the picture makes absolutely sure by turning this briefly into a horror movie. Alexander and Achilles go at it for the sovereign state of Alaska and our boy knocks down the enemy. Does Alexander deliberately fire his rocket fist at the bleachers where hundreds of onlookers are watching the battle unfold? Who knows, but Achilles certainly tries to stop it getting to them by jumping in its way. Sadly, that altruistic act backfires and both he and his giant machine body tumble backwards to squelch them all where they sit. Over three hundred spectators die there in the stands and Achilles is mortified at the sight, which is why, when the officials rule the fight a draw, he refuses to take part in the rematch scheduled for one week later. Alexander laughs at him and calls him a coward. Three hundred bystander corpses mean nothing to him! So yeah, we're on the side of the guy who won't fight any more because he's fought his ten fights and he's done.

Oh, and I have to add that these officials have a notably brutal sense of humour. They just watched three hundred innocent civilians be crushed and they decide to stage the rematch in Death Valley. Ouch! That's harsh! I guess Tombstone was booked up in advance and the Skeleton Coast was too far to travel. It's Alexander we're supposed to be demonising here and

his unseen Confederation masters, not the officials of the Tribunal. I think old Alex missed a trick, though, by not entering Death Valley to the accompaniment of Frank Sinatra's *I've Got a Crush on You*. That would have kept the hate on him!

Anyway, Achilles pronouncing that match his last stand means that the Market are really up against it. He's the last robot jock—Wikipedia seems to believe that the singular of "jox" is also "jox" but I just don't buy it—left on the Market's roster because Alexander's been steadily killing them all. With Achilles gone, it's down to Prof. Laplace's experimental collection of genetically engineered fighters, "gen jox", or, as most seem to call them, "test tube babies", but they aren't ready yet. And, to complicate matters, the reason that the Market is in such dire straits to begin with is that the Confederation keeps figuring out in advance just what secret weapons Dr. Matsumoto is designing into the next machines. The only explanation is that there's a Confed spy somewhere in their midst and there's no time left to figure out who it might be.

That's not a bad story to underpin what might easily be (and generally was) dismissed as a cheap sci-fi flick, but just look at the names involved. The story was conjured up by Stuart Gordon, who wrote and directed the glorious *Re-Animator* in 1985. The script was written by Joe Haldeman, who won the Hugo, Nebula and Locus awards for his 1974 novel, *The Forever War*, and kept on winning after that. This was his only screenplay and he

fought hard to keep his vision intact within it. He has memorably defined it as "a child who started out well and then sustained brain damage." He summed up his differences with Gordon as well, suggesting that he was "writing a movie for adults that children can enjoy" while Gordon was "directing a movie for children that adults can enjoy."

It's easy to see both those approaches in play here and they do ably explain some of the film's schizophrenia. One minute, Achilles, his career over, is welcomed back home by his family. They tell him, "We're having real meat tonight to celebrate," and that means one solitary hot dog. Hey, it's the post-apocalypse, remember, and, even if we've entirely forgotten about that, there are little details there to remind us if we pay attention. The next minute, we're having a giant mecha battle, every one of which has thus far been confined to a single location (hence the ability to sell tickets to spectators), leap off into space where they fight without any of the usual connections to home base. There's absolutely no reason for this, but hey, it's spectacular! It's not difficult to see the former as Haldeman's work and the latter as Gordon's.

The thing is that, when clashes like this happen, someone with talent is usually being jerked around by someone without. Marketing says this. The studio boss says that. The executive producer says the other. Here, it's not like that. Both Gordon and Haldeman are massively talented writers; they were just doing different things with this film and it both benefitted and

The Awesomely Awful '80s, Part 2

suffered from that. Watch it as a kids film and you'll find surprising depth. Watch it as an adult film and you'll find yourself grinning at the crazy bits that make no sense but are still fun.

At the time, of course, the initial inspiration sprung from *Transformers* toys, Gordon wanting to bring giant robots into a live action movie for the very first time. More specifically, he planned to "take advantage of the special effects that are available today"—today being 1987 when they shot this (it took a few years to get released because Empire Pictures went bankrupt before it could initially do so). Given that the *Transformers* films, once they finally got going, took advantage of the much more advanced special effects that were available twenty years on, it's sad to point out that they weren't this much fun.

Maybe it's because I'm a child of the eighties that I grin at this picture so much. Everything here is beautifully analogue and it sets my nostalgia bone a-tinglin'. The phones are massive and the screens are tiny. I haven't seen this many CRTs in far too long! Sure, it's prehistoric technology to the current generation, but mine knows that it should always have weight to keep it anchored in reality.

The suits the jox wear have clunky seventies style designs but they're functional and the giant mecha are fantastic models animated through old school stop motion techniques. I absolutely adored the imaginative design that went into the model work, especially on the Confederation's side—the

bad guys always get the best designs! Sure, there were transforming car robots fighting on top of dinosaur robots over the exploding streets of Hong Kong in one of those insanely boring *Transformers* CGI fests (was that *Age of Extinction*?) but Alexander's mecha has a detachable rocket fist and a frickin' crotch chainsaw! No, mum, I don't want Bumblebee for Christmas! I want Alexander's Confederation mecha with a detachable rocket fist and a crotch chainsaw! You know, from *Robot Jox*!

I'd even settle for a toy of the rattle room training set. The gen jox are given a bizarre session here, a race to escape the room through the hole in the ceiling. In between them and the hole is what's perhaps best described as an upside down climbing frame. Get through first, you win. "When you hear the buzzer, try to make it to the top," explains the instructor. "And stay alive." He isn't kidding either. Some of the bars are red hot, others are slippery because they spray oil. Some just fall off when you touch them. It's a deliberately sabotaged vertical obstacle course and that would have made a fantastic playset!

I should distract myself from this way of thinking by pointing out that Athena wins by virtue of not dying and that makes her the new number one, the successor to Achilles and the new opponent for Alexander's final match, as well as the starting point for a whole new section of story. She's tough and Anne-Marie Johnson, a young African American actress, was a very appropriate casting choice for Athena, the most successful of the first

generation of genetically engineered robot jox. There's prejudice in play here, but it's never to her skin colour, about which nobody cares a whit. I'd have been happier if it was all aimed at her origin as an artificially created human being, thus making us notice the comparisons ourselves, but sadly there's some sexist banter that should have been avoided. Like I said, it's a schizophrenic script.

Perhaps the worst part of this unfortunate schizophrenia is the clash between the gung ho tone of the robot jox, sourced from military chatter, and the anti-war sentiment that underpins the picture. That's what really doesn't work and it leads to inevitable schizophrenia in our response to it. I love this film but I hate this film too and that's unfortunate. But hey, at least I love it a lot more than I do the big budget *Transformers* cinematic abortions. I'll take this one over that entire franchise any day.

Crash and burn, baby! Crash and burn!

The Awesomely Awful '80s, Part 2

The Awesomely Awful '80s, Part 2

The Awesomely Awful '80s, Part 2

See No Evil, Hear No Evil

Director: Arthur Hiller
Writers: Earl Barrett, Arne Sultan, Eliot Wald, Andrew Kurtzman and Gene Wilder, based on a story by Earl Barret, Arne Sultan and Marvin Worth
Stars: Richard Pryor, Gene Wilder, Joan Severance, Kevin Spacey, Alan North, Anthony Zerbe, Louis Giambalvo and Kirsten Childs

This forgotten feature begins like any other from the era. Music that's recognisably Stewart Copeland's, when we'd almost forgotten that he had just been in a huge pop band. The Twin Towers, seen prominently over the Brooklyn bridge. New Yorkers bitching emphatically at each other for no reason over the tumultuous noise of roadwork and sirens. Gene Wilder almost getting run over because he's deaf. Wait, what? Yeah, you heard that right! Ah crap, it's not going to be easy to avoid puns in this one.

Yes, someone—and there are so many names credited for writing this script, five people adapting a story by three of them, that we have no idea who to blame—thought it might be a good idea to make a film about a deaf guy. And a blind guy. A deaf and a blind guy bound together by the chains of circumstance and struggling to communicate, let alone escape from the intrigue into which they've been unceremoniously dumped. Oh, and those writers? They made it a comedy. Now how could that possibly go wrong?

Well, the names behind it are important ones. The director is Arthur Hiller, who had been nominated for a Primetime Emmy as far back as 1962 for directing episodes of *Naked City*. His Oscar nod was for 1971's *Love Story* but he had a strong career directing pictures as wildly varied as *Tobruk*, *Author! Author!* and *Silver Streak*, the first of four big movies to team Wilder with Richard Pryor—this film is the third, with *Stir Crazy* in between and *Another You* still to come. These are greatly talented people. Why any of them felt like men missing senses were suitable fodder for a mainstream comedy, I have no idea.

Oh and yes, your logic is correct. If Wilder is playing the deaf guy, Wally Carew by name, then Pryor must be playing the blind guy, David Lyons, right? You got it. This odd couple meet right at the start of the film and... well, that's not strictly true; they only sort of meet right at the start of the film because that's how the humour is built.

Remember I mentioned that Gene Wilder almost got run over? Well, a driver showed polite concern towards him when he didn't respond to his driving towards him. By polite concern, of course, I mean honking his horn like a madman and yelling "What are you, deaf?" because he's a New Yorker and he can't honestly believe that the person acting like he's deaf might actually be deaf. Are all New Yorkers really like Hollywood tells us they are? It seems unlikely. Of course, if they are, all Australians must be lovable adventurers like "Crocodile" Dundee and all we Brits must be well spoken villains like Hans Gruber. Again, I don't think so, but that would be cool. Let's test. "I'm going to count to three, there won't be a four... Give me the code." Yeah, that feels rather good, if I do say so myself! "Do you really think you have a chance against us, Mr. Cowboy?"

Anyway, when Wally finally notices this oncoming truck and jumps out of the way, the driver yells, "You dumb idiot!" and he notices that because he's looking right at him, so he responds in kind. "*You're* a dumb idiot!" he shouts, pointing at the driver, and David, emerging from the subway, like

The Awesomely Awful '80s, Part 2

every New Yorker is contractually obligated to do at some point in every movie, thinks he's talking to him instead because, you know, he's as blind as a bat. Now that doesn't stop him responding physically, but his flailing punches don't reach Wally because he can't see him and Wally has no idea he's doing it because he's looking the other way and can't hear a word he's saying. And, quite frankly, riffs on this theme are what we get for the next hundred minutes until the end credits roll.

In fact, I can explain the entire movie just by setting a few scenes. Like the one where David tries to get a job working for Wally at his concession shop in a hotel. You can imagine how that goes: for half the conversation, Wally is blissfully unaware that there is a conversation, and for the other half, he's lost because he wasn't there for the first half. Or the one where David picks a fight in a bar and Wally helps him out by directing each of his punches. "Aim for twelve o'clock!" Or, most importantly, how about the one where Joan Severance shows up and murders David's bookie right there at Wally's kiosk. That's what sets everything else in motion.

You see, the MacGuffin of the piece is a coin—which turns out to not be a coin, but that's really not important—which is cunningly concealed in a secret compartment in the bookie's briefcase. He's aware that he's being pursued for it so he has Wally turn around and read him the directions on a box of Di-Gel as a distraction while he slips the coin into the cigar box used for tips. By the time he turns back, the bookie is dead, shot during a

struggle with Eve, Severance's character, who's looking for the coin. Wally only sees her memorable legs walking away with the briefcase; they, along with the Shalimar fragrance David smells as he passes her on the way into the building, become all they have to go on as the primary witnesses to a murder that, well, neither technically witnessed.

You'd think that New York's finest would soon sort that out, but it turns out that Capt. Braddock, in charge of the investigation, is played by Alan North, whom you'll recognise from his notably similar role in *Police Squad!* He's not quite as inept here but he's inept enough for Wally and David to feel the need to escape his custody, as he sees them as suspects rather than witnesses. And so we're off and running, with Wally and David as the good guys, Eve and her employers as the bad guys and the entire NYPD as the idiots in the middle.

Here's where I point out that I was surprised in a few different ways by a fresh viewing. For one, Kevin Spacey is in the film, playing Eve's partner, Kirgo. Of course, being the villain, he's young and has a weasel moustache and a suave British accent. See what I mean about Hollywood now? What's weirdest here is that I must have seen Spacey in a whole bunch of movies growing up but I don't remember him before the mid-nineties. *Se7en* and *The Usual Suspects*, those are where my brain tells me his career began but no, he was in *Working Girl* and *Dad* and *See No Evil, Hear No Evil*, doing a sort of proto-Kevin Spacey act. At least, that's how it seems to me now.

The Awesomely Awful '80s, Part 2

For another, I originally saw this movie on British television, before the nine o'clock watershed, which means that I had absolutely no idea that it contained any swearing. Yeah, I know, it stars Richard Pryor; what was I thinking? Well, I must have seen a TV edit that made it family friendly and it's far from that in its original form. Watching this in 2018 made me feel like the Mormon who loved *My Cousin Vinny* so much as an inflight movie that he rented it to show the wife and kids; he discovered that the original version also starred Joe Pesci.

What's strangest of all is that I'm sure that I remember Joan Severance's boobs, which really shouldn't have been in a family friendly TV edit. They are rather memorable, though they also may have earned as many credits as she did over the years. I'm pretty sure I did see them, because they're the most likely reason for me to remember this picture as anything other than a train wreck, unless my sense of humour was wildly immature when I was eighteen. Yeah, come to think of it...

Well, my sense of humour has matured far enough that I know that this film is wildly inappropriate, politically incorrect in the extreme and quite obvious in its use of humour. For instance, what's the obvious thing you'd have a blind man and a deaf man do after escaping police custody? That's right! They'd steal a police car and drive it the wrong way down a one way street. With the blind guy at the wheel. "Watch the road!" pleads Wally. "If it makes you feel better," replies David. I can't help but laugh at this scene,

however inappropriate it is, because it's the pinnacle of surreality in a film whose very concept is surreal.

The most ridiculous scene has to be the one where they track Kirgo and Eve to the Great Gorge resort, in search of the coin that the bad guys have managed to acquire from them. The hotel is all booked up, because of a medical conference, so they manage to get in by pretending to be foreign doctors. I am well aware that there may well be black doctors in Sweden, but I'm guessing that none of them are called Dr. Johansen. And yes, he's a gynecologist; you're way ahead of me here! Of course he gets dragged into a room to speak at a seminar, but Wally rescues him by pretending that he has "blindness hysteria". It's all as incredibly stupid as you're imagining. "Who are you, sir?" "Fine, thank you." I much preferred the boob shot.

The sad thing is that there are points where the jokes are both funny and insightful, not to mention sensitive. There's a fantastic scene early in the picture when Wally and David are arrested and the cops grill them for information. Braddock rattles off a question so quickly that Wally can't tell what he says. David tells him to slow down because he's reading his lips, so he slows way down and Wally reacts the same way. "Why's he talking like that?" Braddock asks. "Because he's deaf, not stupid," replies David.

That's good humour and there are other scenes that match it. There's one almost at the beginning when Mr. Huddleston, the doorman at the hotel where Wally has his concession shop, tries to explain to him in baby

language that the fire inspector wants him to sweep up. Wally's response is to attempt to quash the vicious rumour floating around that he's deaf. Huddleston buys it and feels terrible. Again, it's good humour but it's also good insight into how people with a missing sense are treated like babies because of it, when they're really regular people who merely can't see or hear or speak, depending on which sense they're missing.

The background of the characters helps this angle too. Wally has come to terms with his deafness, which was caused by a bout of scarlet fever in high school, so prompting a gradual loss of hearing. He lost it completely only eight years prior, which was when his wife left. She turned into a witch at the same time as he went deaf. How about that? David, however, hasn't come to terms with anything. He lost his sight when a drunk driver forced him into a fire hydrant. He refuses to accept his blindness, pretending to read the newspaper on the subway and avoiding the use of a cane. At one point, he even helps another blind man across the street into the back of a delivery truck. There is depth here.

Needless to say, the film would have been a lot better if there had been more exploration of how Wally and David interact with the world around them and more scenes like the ones where the world tries and often fails to interact back. Instead, of course, we're dumped onto the front row for Dr. Johansen's gynecological insights. It would have been a better movie too if Richard Pryor didn't spend the entire running time with a shocked

expression on his face as if someone had attached a car battery to his testicles. If he wants people to stop treating him like he's blind, then it would seem appropriate to not scream that at the world.

I liked Wilder as Wally—of course, Gene Wilder is perhaps the easiest actor in history to like, whatever his role—but I didn't like Pryor as David, physically at least. I think he would have been a lot better on radio and that's not a crack at the blind. Just because I can't help but wonder how the captioned version of this film worked for a hearing impaired audience doesn't mean I'm prejudiced. I just believe the film is and I'm interested in the opinion of audience members who might share the experience of the two lead characters.

"I feel ridiculous," says the deaf guy. "You look fine to me," replies the blind guy. That's objectively funny and whether you think it's appropriate to build a comedy out of it will determine whether you're going to like this film or not. Of course, you didn't need two thousand words to help you decide that. You'd have figured it out by the end of paragraph two.

The Awesomely Awful '80s, Part 2

The Awesomely Awful '80s, Part 2

… The Awesomely Awful '80s, Part 2 …

Road House

Director: Rowdy Herrington
Writers: David Lee Henry and Hilary Henkin, from a story by David Lee Henry.
Stars: Patrick Swayze, Kelly Lynch, Kevin Tighe, Keith David, Kathlee Wilhoite, "Sunshine" Parker, Red West, Julie Michaels and Sam Elliott

Picture a world, Rod Serling might say, where bouncers are superstars and their names are spoken in hushed tones across the land. Yeah, this is hardly the most realistic feature ever made but it's a good contender for the most entertaining and it's a heck of a lot better than the previous film with a major Hollywood name in a surprising screen occupation. No, Tom Cruise, bartenders aren't superstars either.

Part of the reason why *Road House* is timeless is because it's hardly new. At heart, it's the same old story we've seen a hundred times before of a big boss in a small town terrorising everyone who lives and works there, with a lone outsider doing something about it. It's a western. It's *Shane*. And I'm not going to argue that it was new then. However, we remember *Shane* for Jack Palance whispering at people to "pick up the gun" and we remember *Road House* for Ben Gazzara swerving all over the road while singing along to *Sh-Boom* by the Crew-Cuts. That's if you're male, of course. If you're not, you're more likely to remember it for Patrick Swayze's naked butt. Either or both; it doesn't matter. *Road House* is archetypal and we remember it.

Swayze is Dalton, because of course he is. He's hardly going to be a Bert or a Timothy with moves like these. Everyone has western names because writer R. Lance Hill, using the pseudonym of David Lee Henry, knew that it was a western at heart. They're Wade and Brad and Emmet, Hank and Red and Cody, Morgan and Pat and Tinker. And he's Dalton, named, I assume, for the Dalton Gang, a band of outlaws who robbed trains in the old west after stints as lawmen, changing jobs because they weren't getting paid. It

The Awesomely Awful '80s, Part 2

actually runs a lot deeper than first names, almost every name in this film being sourced from the Wild West, but that's an article all of its own.

Dalton gets paid well because he's the best in the business, or so Frank Tilghman tells him. He owns the Double Deuce, a club in the small town of Jasper, MO, a couple of hours south of Kansas City; he's come into some money and he wants to clean it up. "Used to be a sweet deal," he explains. "Now it's the kind of place they sweep up the eyeballs after closing." And so Dalton drives down to take care of business.

I say drives, because Dalton doesn't fly. It's too risky, he says and he's an inveterate risk assessor because of his job. That's obvious from our very first look at him, an oasis of calm in a busy club, watching every move and every reaction, looking for signs of trouble. Of course, he still smokes like a chimney, because who says he has to be consistent? It was cool when the westerns this apes were popular, so it's cool now, right? He's a man out of his time, that's all, hanging out with the Marlboro Man in his dreams.

Well, the Double Deuce needs someone who's a lot more than cool, as Tilghman really wasn't overstating the case. You know it's a tough joint when the stage is enclosed by chicken wire, but that's just the start. There are loud bikers outside and grabby customers inside. There are waitresses dealing drugs, customers sleeping on the floor, fights breaking all over the place. The bouncers are kept very busy. Bottles are broken all over, even when they're not being thrown at the stage.

Oh, and there are insanely bad chat up lines. I quite liked, "I get off at two and I'd just love to get you off about a half hour after that." Nice. My

The Awesomely Awful '80s, Part 2

favourite, though, is, "Hey Vodka Rocks, what do you say you and me get nipple to nipple?" The reply, from a quintessential buxom blonde is, "I can do that without you." The most shocking thing about this movie may be the fact that Denise, this vapid blonde bimbo, is much better known nowadays as a stunt coordinator of note, a career that has since led her to an Emmy nomination, than an actress. She's Julie Michaels and she's also a writer and producer. When Wade Garrett says, "That gal's got entirely too many brains to have an ass like that," he's emphatically not talking about Denise, but the line could easily apply to Julie Michaels herself.

It feels appropriate to mention this right now because, pausing to take stock after the inevitable Double Deuce bar fight to wrap up the evening, I realised that, only fifteen minutes in, this testosterone-fuelled action flick has already given more women dialogue than the entire running times of *Bloodsport* and *Action Jackson* put together. It even gave them things to do during that bar fight; there were quite a few ladies right there in the thick of the action, whether staff or customers, throwing punches of their own and hitting people over the head with bottles. Hey, maybe the women are here for something other than just that Swayze butt shot after all!

In fact, while the action is plentiful, there's a spiritual side to this movie that resonates. I'm not talking about a topless Swayze running through his tai chi forms, I'm talking about Dalton driving out by the river and taking a room above old Emmet's barn. It has no phone, no television, no AC, "no tolerance from the fragrance of nature," as the farmer memorably puts it, but he takes it anyway because he's the simple man who lives a simple life

and, to my thinking, that makes this film work as much as putting the Jeff Healey Band behind that chicken wire on the Double Deuce stage. It's one more way to highlight what separates Dalton from Brad Wesley, the boss of this town: not only their moral code, but the river and their way of life.

Now, the philosophy isn't particularly deep, even if Dalton has a degree in "man's search for faith, that sort of shit." He comes out with dialogue as deep and meaningful as "Pain don't hurt" and "Nobody ever wins a fight", not to mention his famous advice to his new staff to "be nice until it's time to not be nice." Heck, this is a movie with a monster truck, a striptease and a stuffed polar bear, so really, how deep was it ever going to get? Well, philosophy and spirituality are not the same thing and I'm sure that a lot of the latter came from the western bedrock of Hill's original story. What I'm wondering now is how much of it came from the fact that he adapted it into a screenplay with a female scriptwriter, Hilary Henkin.

It certainly wouldn't surprise me to learn that the romantic side of the film was predominantly her work, as it's not what we usually see in action movies, even if Dalton and Doc meet when he goes to hospital to get his side stapled shut after a knife sliced it open and she's assigned to the job. For a start, the romance is actually romantic! I know, stop the presses! Next thing you know, their ensuing relationship won't be defined by how good they each are in the sack. And they'll talk to each other. And, well, this one goes all the way to the point where she gets to be a character in her own right! Wow, that almost never happens! At points, it actually seems to be trying not to be just a testosterone-fuelled movie.

Now, to be fair, she's not a particularly important character in her own right. She is mostly defined by her relationships (to Dalton, to her father and to Brad Wesley) and I don't believe that she ever talks to anyone of the same gender at any point in the picture. Now, it's hardly unusual for an action flick to fail the Bechdel Test, where two female characters have to talk about something other than a man, but this one doesn't even have her talk to a female character, period. There's even a female nurse who help her prepare for stapling and she doesn't even speak to her. Not even a single word of thanks. Yes, I checked. I'm a professional, after all, even if Doc isn't. One of the other nurses does say hi to her, but she doesn't reply. There must be a strict pecking order at her hospital or something.

Still, Doc is no waste of space. Take Sydney Ash out of *Action Jackson* and nobody would care. Take Janice Kent out of *Bloodsport* and nobody would even notice. Take Doc out of *Road House* and you have a whole new movie and that's more than a little refreshing. Of course, it doesn't hurt for Kelly Lynch to have some chemistry with Swayze and the two of them to have a sensual sex scene up above the barn where there's no tolerance from the fragrance of nature, even if it's to the requisite soul number on the radio. I was as impressed by this scene as I was distracted by how much of an outie Patrick Swayze has. Maybe that's why Dalton learned how to stitch up his own wounds; he's had bad experiences with the medical profession.

Now, there is another reason why women watch *Road House* and that's easily summed up in two words: Sam and Elliott. He's one of those lucky men who makes most ladies melt on sight and the ones who don't tend to

The Awesomely Awful '80s, Part 2

follow suit once he opens his mouth. What's odd is that he seems—how do I phrase this politely?—old. He was 45 at the time, eight years older than Swayze, so it makes sense that he look older but he looks more likely to be a contemporary of Ben Gazzara, who played Brad Wesley at the age of 59. Elliott even looks older than Terry Funk who, as a professional wrestler of renown, ought to look damaged, but he was actually a couple of months younger. Funk, by the way, plays Morgan, the massive bouncer that Dalton fires from the Double Douce, whom waitress Carrie Ann memorably sums up: "Morgan was born an asshole and just grew bigger."

However old Elliott looks, Wade Garrett does epitomise the man who's been there and done that. He's grizzled and tough and as good at flirting with Dalton's girl as helping him out in a fight. He's a good friend and he's also the one bouncer higher up the list of legendary bouncers than Dalton. I'd love to see that list, by the way. Is it documented in the back of *Cooler Monthly* like a *Billboard* chart? What criteria do they use to classify these legends? Number of days at work without an accident? Count of teenage girls with their centerfold posters from *Tiger Beat* pinned to their bedroom walls? The sheer depth of their licensed tie-in product lines? Do Japanese schoolgirls buy pairs of Dalton socks or Wade Garrett plushies? You know, I'm starting to call foul on this legendary bouncer thing, folks, I'm sorry.

Anyway, Brad Wesley turns out to be extra-ruthless so Garrett comes to Jasper to help his buddy out. You know, if our two sexy tough guys get to be legendary bouncers, does that mean that Brad Wesley has a fame of his own in *Small Town Big Boss* magazine? Where does he stand on the local

The Awesomely Awful '80s, Part 2

despot chart? I'm guessing above the many corrupt hicks of the week on *The A-Team*, but above or below Boss Hogg? He doesn't have a Boar's Nest but he does have a helicopter and a trophy room and both billiards and pool tables. He has a pet blonde and a pet thug, with the requisite earring. And of course, he has the local authorities under his thumb, so much so that we don't see a one of them until the finalé plays out in full. Wouldn't it be great to see a boss ranking generated by vote when every one of the candidates is as corrupt as the next and they're all bribing each other? I'd tune in for that reality TV show, that's for sure!

Of course, with Dalton standing up to Brad Wesley—it just doesn't seem right to use only one of his names—the rest of the townsfolk start to do likewise. And, of course, things then start to happen. You've seen this plot so many times I don't need to dig any deeper, but it's done with emphatic style here, with buildings exploding and monster trucks crushing and coin tosses over the phone tormenting. "It's my town," he tells people, but in a way we believe because Ben Gazzara rocks the role. I've seen him in a few other movies but it's hard to imagine him any other way but this, hitting his employees and then complaining that they bleed. He's as iconic and as defining as the rest of the movie.

The best commentary I've read on *Road House* came from Kelly Lynch, who plays Doc,. She talked about her experiences rocking her tablecloth mini-skirt in an interview with Will Harris of the AV Club. According to her, Rowdy Herrington, the director, was trying to make "the best drive-in movie ever made" and the cast were in on the joke. They roared at every

over-the-top line when the camera wasn't on but played them straight as they were meant to. She also talks about how the film has lived on in wild ways, like how Bill Murray or "one of his idiot brothers" always calls her husband whenever *Road House* is on television. "Hi, Kelly's having sex with Patrick Swayze right now."

In short, it's fun. It's a heck of a lot of fun, even though it falls apart at the slightest analysis. The population of Jasper in 1989 was just short of a thousand people and 20% were under eighteen. Who does Frank Tilghman think is going to show up to his remodelled Double Deuce? Is he planning to steal them away from the bright lights of Joplin? You'd think that he'd get better bang for the buck by hiring a hitman to take down Brad Wesley with all that money he's come into. But hey, I'm delving. Next I'll start to wonder how Dalton can fight these fights without ever breaking open his staples, even when Jimmy the earring dude slams him in the side with a frickin' tree. Are these magic staples? How much extra do they cost?

I'm going to close out, not just this review but this book, by quoting a line from the Jeff Healey Band's final song, the best one in the film and the one that plays out over the closing credits. It's a fantastic cover of Bob Dylan's *When the Night Comes Falling from the Sky* and it includes this line: "I know that you were flirting with disaster, somehow managed to escape."

To me, that sums up *Road House* perfectly, because it really shouldn't be this much fun, and, by extension, it does a pretty good job of summing up the other movies I've had fun exploring for this book. All of them ought to be disasters but maybe some of them somehow managed to escape.

The Awesomely Awful '80s, Part 2

Bibliography

Research for this book, like my others, started with Wikipedia and IMDb and continued on from there. I've cited some sources within the articles but the following articles and interviews were especially useful. I highly recommend checking them out:

How Did This Get Made: A Conversation with Mel Brooks, Executive Producer of 'Solarbabies' by Blake Harris

> https://www.slashfilm.com/mel-brooks-interview/3/

Remaking The Gate: *Interview Alex Winter (English Version)* by

> http://www.screenread.de/the-gate-3d-alex-winter-interview-english/

Is That Your First Name or Your Last Name?: Remembering Deathstalker 2 *with Jim Wynorski* by Kent Hill

> https://podcastingthemsoftly.com/2016/11/15/is-that-your-first-name-or-your-last-name-remembering-deathstalker-2-with-jim-wynorski-by-kent-hill/

Playboy Playmates, Penthouse Pets, and Parallel Realities: The Comic Book World of Cult Filmmaker Andy Sidaris by Jason Coffman

> https://medium.com/applaudience/playboy-playmates-penthouse-pets-and-parallel-realities-the-comic-book-world-of-cult-filmmaker-ad0ccf614f3e

NINJA: Hero or Master Fake?: Others Kick Holes in Fabled Past of Woodland Hills Martial Arts Teacher by John Johnson

> https://www.latimes.com/archives/la-xpm-1988-05-01-me-3111-story.html

The Sales Games Played by Nintendo's Wizard by Anthony Ramirez

> https://www.nytimes.com/1989/12/21/business/the-games-played-for-nintendo-s-sales.html

Kelly Lynch on Magic City, *John Hughes, and playing a drag king* by Will Harris

> https://film.avclub.com/kelly-lynch-on-magic-city-john-hughes-and-playing-a-d-1798234234

The Awesomely Awful '80s, Part 2

About Hal C. F. Astell

While he still has a day job to pay the bills, Hal C. F. Astell is a teacher by blood and a writer by the grace of the dread lord, which gradually transformed him into a film critic. He reviews films and music at Apocalypse Later and books for the Nameless Zine.

Born and raised in the rain of England, he's still learning about the word "heat" over a decade after he emigrated to Phoenix, AZ, where he lives with Dee, his much better half, in a house full of assorted critters and oddities, a library with a guard ferret and more obscure DVDs than can comfortably be imagined. And he can imagine quite a lot. What he'd like for Christmas is time to watch them.

Just in case you care, his favourite movie is Peter Jackson's debut, *Bad Taste*, his favourite actor is Warren William and he thinks Carl Theodor Dreyer's *The Passion of Joan of Arc* is the greatest movie ever made. He's always happy to talk your ears off about the joys of odd and interesting films and their makers, whether they're pre-codes, fifties B-movies, obscure Asian horror flicks or whatever.

He's usually easy to find at film festivals, conventions and events because he's likely to be the only one there in a kilt and his fading English accent is instantly recognisable on podcasts and panels. He is friendly and doesn't bite unless asked.

Photo Credit: Dee Astell

The Awesomely Awful '80s, Part 2

About Apocalypse Later

Initially, Hal C. F. Astell wrote film reviews for his own reference because he could never remember who the one good actor was in otherwise forgettable entries in long crime series from the forties. After a year, they became long enough to warrant a dedicated blog.

The name came from an abandoned project in which he aimed to review his way through the entire IMDb Top 250. Its tentative title was a joke sourced from the idea of reviewing *Apocalypse Now* last.

Gradually he focused on writing about the sort of films that most critics don't, avoiding adverts, scripts, monetisation and the eye-killing horror of white text on a black background.

Four million words later and Apocalypse Later Press was born, to publish his first book, cunningly titled *Huh?* This growth eventually became the Apocalypse Later Empire, which now includes a review site, a publishing imprint, a blog, a roadshow at conventions across the American southwest, a Facebook group about steampunk film and a full dedicated annual genre film festival in Phoenix: ALIFFF, the Apocalypse Later International Fantastic Film Festival, which was launched in 2016.

Apocalypse Later celebrated its tenth anniversary in 2017.

Hop in your time machine
and I'll see you sometime for

The Awesomely Awful '80s, Part 1

www.ingramcontent.com/pod-product-compliance
Lightning Source LLC
LaVergne TN
LVHW051545070426
835507LV00021B/2422